# Three Minute Therapy

# Three Minute Therapy:
## *Change Your Thinking, Change Your Life*

**Michael R. Edelstein, Ph.D.**

**and David Ramsay Steele, Ph.D.**

Gallatin House

Dr. Edelstein's e-mail & website:
DrEdelstein@ThreeMinuteTherapy.com
http://www.threeminutetherapy.com

*Three Minute Therapy* was first published in 1997 in a clothbound edition by Glenbridge Publishing Ltd., of Aurora, Colorado. This new paperback edition, with some additional material, was first published in 2019 by Gallatin House of San Francisco.

International Standard Book Number:
978-0-359-07193-7

Printed in the U.S.A.

Cover design by Thomas Rossini

# Contents

# *Foreword*

In my long career as a therapist I am reminded continually that just about all people are both born and reared with neurotic tendencies. They have ample opportunity to rehearse these dysfunctional actions, which are practiced both consciously and unconsciously, before they think seriously of reducing them. Most resist giving up their disturbances, even when they see how destructive they are. They have already developed a low frustration tolerance and are unwilling to work with sufficient energy to change themselves.

Of course, it takes significantly longer than three minutes to dislodge the many dysfunctional aspects of a troubled personality. But the clear and simple exercises advocated by Dr. Edelstein, exercises that are totally consistent with my principles of Rational Emotive Behavior Therapy, can be practiced in three-minute segments, to be repeated several times a day for maximum benefit.

Most people do not know how to change their neurotic thoughts and actions in order to reduce their disturbed feelings. I witnessed this in my patients after I had practiced as a psychoanalyst for six years in the early 1950s. I created Rational Emotive Behavior Therapy in order to solve this important problem in my practice and began using the system in January of 1955. It became quickly apparent that this system was a highly efficient form of psychotherapy that, over time, quickly identified problems in thousands of my patients. As Drs. Edelstein and Steele so ably point out, the three-minute exercises must be practiced regularly and conscientiously, and in serious cases, perhaps for years, since it probably took many years for those seriously disturbed to develop the dysfunctional or neurotic thought patterns that have created the problems.

As humans, we seem to have a talent for disturbing ourselves about innumerable unpleasant events that occur in our lives. We then may react to these "adversities" by making ourselves feel sorry, displeased, or disappointed—all normal reactions. But then we may also feel panicked, depressed, enraged, self-downing, and self-pitying about these unfortunate life experiences, reactions likely to make us miserable and to send us to a therapist for help.

REBT shows you, clearly and precisely, how you needlessly and unhealthily upset yourself, and it gives you many thinking, feeling, and action methods of reducing your disturbances while still retaining your main goals, values, and preferences. If you keep using these methods, you are more likely to be less disturbed and less "disturbable." There are no magic solutions, however, only serious effort.

But as Drs. Edelstein and Steele emphasize, *starting* to "undisturb" yourself whenever you are really upset can usually be done in three minutes. *Continuing* to do so takes longer. With the good head start offered in *Three Minute Therapy* you can be well on your way.

Of all the books that explain REBT in simple, clear, and highly usable form, *Three Minute Therapy* is one of the very best. The authors include the main theories and practices of REBT and specifically tell you how to apply them to your own problems. No, this is not a self-help encyclopedia, but it tells you almost everything you will want to know about using REBT in your own life. Read it carefully, several times. Try its methods, many times. Practice is essential.

Every time you heed its three-minute approach you may start to add months and years of healthier and happier existence to your living. Try it and see!

Albert Ellis, Ph.D.

# Preface: What This Book Can Do For You

This book cannot solve all your problems. But it can help you change your life dramatically for the better.

If you read *Three Minute Therapy* and consider what it says, you will find yourself looking at the world in a different way. Emotional troubles—your own and other people's—will seem less mysterious and less powerful. You will understand that a great deal of advice offered by many therapists and counselors often only makes matters worse.

If you take the trouble to learn the techniques explained in this book, think about them, and apply them to your own problems, you'll be able to tackle difficulties that may have so far seemed unmanageable. Some of your worst fears and anxieties will diminish or dissolve away, and you will become more effective at pursuing your chosen goals in life.

We call this book *Three Minute Therapy* because, once you have learned these techniques, you can then cope with most emotional problems by employing a Three Minute Exercise. Actually, to learn the techniques and the theory behind them will take a little longer—say, three hours to read this book, and three weeks to think it over.

The theory underlying this book is that of Rational Emotive Behavior Therapy (REBT), originated by Albert Ellis who deserves the credit for undertaking a revolution in psychotherapy. We have developed our own fresh way of explaining the exciting principles of REBT so that they become as vivid and simple as possible.

The case histories cited are all drawn from Dr. Edelstein's clinical experience. Names and other personal details have been changed, and in some instances details of two or more different clients have been combined in one composite personality. Both authors had some input on every page of this book; in most cases, the fundamental ideas came from Dr. Edelstein and the precise wording was a joint effort. "We" refers to both authors, while "I" always refers to Dr. Edelstein.

# *Acknowledgments*

A number of our colleagues, friends, and family were gracious enough to read and comment on drafts of this book: John Bassett, Michael Behre, Walter Block, Jamie Davis, Bernice Douglas, Louise Dubberke, Janice Edelstein, Albert Ellis, Michele Hubinger, Joseph S. Lowenstein, Nando Pelusi, Roberta Rosen, Chris Rossini, "AO" Sachs, Jerome Tarshis, Emmett Velten, Robert Wenzel, Martín Zapata, and Lisa Zimmerman.

# 1

## Ending Your Self-Inflicted Pain

> *What upsets people is not things themselves but their judgments about the things.*
> —EPICTETUS (ca. A.D. 50–130)

Nearly everything in this book flows from a single, simple fact: the way you feel, emotionally, arises from the way you think. *Your feelings come from your thinking.* For most people, this truth is usually overlooked or denied. Here are some typical statements from my clients:

"I'm furious 'cause my eight-year-old didn't get to bed last night until 1 A.M."

"I'm awfully afraid Jim won't show up for this appointment" (spoken by Jim's wife while waiting for her husband in my office).

"One impossible deadline after another. No wonder I'm so stressed out when I get home from work."

"I've just discovered that my husband and my best friend have been carrying on for three weeks while lying to my face" (spoken by a wife, to explain her feelings of terrible injury and jealousy).

"My husband never talks to me: I'm so depressed."

"I was raised by two alcoholic parents. No wonder I'm an alcoholic."

All these statements suggest that when something happens to you, when some event occurs in your life, that happening or event is sufficient to explain how you feel about it.

What these people are really saying is that exposure to a keenly obnoxious, disagreeable *Activating event* (we'll call this event "A") directly causes the emotional *Consequence* (call this "C"). These clients—along with most people—are expressing their view that there is a direct link between A and C, the unpleasant situation and their upset feeling.

## Your Thoughts and Your Feelings

This is a very popular theory, but it's a *false* theory. Events do not directly affect our psyches the way a needle in the arm causes pain (even then the pain has to go through our brain before we can feel it).

To get a glimpse of the correct theory, imagine that you are about to enter a room where someone awaits you. Your emotions will be related to your *preconceptions*, your thoughts or *Beliefs* (which we'll refer to as "B").

If you expect a violent criminal, you may very well feel afraid. If instead you anticipate that it's your young child who has been missing for days, you're likely to feel greatly relieved and overjoyed.

However, your beliefs, expectations, and anticipations—your B's—are things that *you* generate and control. And it's B that creates C: beliefs create emotions. A or the Activating event alone does not create emotions.

Suppose a hundred airplane passengers are unexpectedly given parachutes and instructed to jump from the plane (A). If a physical situation alone could cause emotions—if A could directly cause C—then all the hundred people would feel the same way. But obviously those who regard skydiving positively (B) are going to have a C very different from the others.

The fact that feelings come from thinking was known to the ancient Greek Stoics and to many Buddhist teachers. It has more recently been rediscovered by Albert Ellis and other psychologists and has been tested in practice by thousands of therapists.

Unfortunately, there are still many therapists and counselors who are either unaware of this fact or who continually deny it. It's not surprising that most ordinary people also deny it.

## *Your Childhood is Irrelevant to Your Present Problems*

Everyone knows that individuals respond very differently to similar events. Jane dreads her upcoming examination so intensely that she can't sleep the night before, and walks into the examination hall shaking with terror. Her friend Barbara, who's taking the same test, remains quite unruffled.

Clearly, a person's response to events is not entirely explained by the events themselves, but owes something to the person. However, instead of looking at that person's conscious *beliefs*, for example Jane's beliefs about the test, therapists often try to explain the person's feelings and actions through their "unconscious" minds.

Sigmund Freud developed this way of explaining human behavior early in the twentieth century, a method popularized by many Hollywood movies from the 1930s on. Freud believed that our feelings and actions are caused by "unconscious" impulses—things that are in our minds but that we don't know about. Our minds are filled with dark, disguised forces of which we're normally quite unaware. How did these mysterious forces get there? They allegedly originated in our childhood experiences.

Jane's fear of the test might be explained by incidents in her early childhood. Freud believed that the way to cure Jane is to uncover the buried memories of those incidents, have Jane relive those incidents, and show how they cause Jane's present anxiety about tests. This excavation of Jane's "unconscious mind" can be a long and expensive process. The therapist encourages the patient to reconstruct some childhood incident, and to accept the therapist's theory about how this is related to the patient's current problems.

This approach to solving people's problems has become very well-known, and many people expect therapists to be interested in the details of their childhood. But there's actually not a scrap of solid evidence that memories of childhood agonies have much to do with a person's continuing emotional difficulties, nor that uncovering those agonies will do anything to help the person now. Even where a person's current problems really are related to a past unpleasant experience, it's the person's present thinking about that experience that does the damage, not the experience itself.

The theory that our feelings and behavior are governed by "unconscious" forces is not only unsubstantiated—it could be harmful. If people with problems believe this theory, they could become demoralized. The theory suggests to people with emotional problems that they are the puppets of dark forces they cannot control or even recognize. Instead of encouraging clients to feel that they are responsible for their problems and that they can do something about them right away, the theory suggests that the individual is helpless, even possessed. The individual is, in effect, encouraged to give up the struggle to be rational and effective.

## *"Shoulds" and "Musts"*

Your feelings come from your thinking. This doesn't mean that if you tell yourself everything is fine and you have no problems, then you will feel fine and your problems will disappear. The *Three Minute Therapy* method does not recommend "thinking positively," telling yourself to cheer up, or fondly dwelling on comfortable images that everything is wonderful.

The advice glibly offered to emotional sufferers— "Worrying doesn't do any good, so why worry?"—is usually of little help because the anxious person doesn't know how to stop worrying. Such a person has a definite system of beliefs, which has become a fixed dogma, and which automatically generates distress. Without attacking and changing that system of beliefs, there will probably be little progress in reducing anxiety. But the sufferer doesn't think much about the system of beliefs, doesn't consider that the beliefs might be questionable, and doesn't notice how the beliefs lead to counterproductive and self-destructive behavior.

To start on the path to healthy thought patterns, it's first necessary to identify the sufferer's system of beliefs. This isn't a lengthy process of excavating "unconscious" memories. Usually a few minutes of asking simple questions will elicit a person's faulty thinking. If someone asks you whether you have a belief about the persistence of physical objects, you will probably be puzzled and hesitate to give a definite reply, or you may even reply in the negative. However, you don't pay much attention to the possibility that the chair you are sitting on will suddenly vanish, causing you to painfully bruise your buttocks on the floor. In this sense, you do indeed subscribe to a belief in the persistence of physical objects, and this belief determines your behavior. In this case, of course, the belief is broadly true.

In the same way, the beliefs responsible for emotional problems are deeply-rooted, unconsidered assumptions. And these beliefs are false. Fortunately, when we wish to identify these beliefs, we start with an advantage. We already have a good idea, on the basis of the theories of Albert Ellis, and the experience of thousands of therapists employing his method, of the mistaken beliefs many people hold.

Such beliefs show a common pattern. They take the form of *demands*—"musts" or "shoulds." For instance, a person faced with a public speaking assignment may believe that he MUST not look foolish in public, and that to do so would be TERRIBLE. While it's reasonable not to want to look foolish in public, it's harmful to *demand* that this be guaranteed not to occur. Thus, the first step in curing public speaking anxiety is to accept, fully and without reservation, that nothing can possibly give you an iron-clad guarantee that you will not look foolish in public. You may possibly look foolish in public—to do so would be unfortunate, but not terrible.

The beliefs that give people emotional problems are evaluative beliefs. Virtually all emotion comes from evaluative thinking. Thus, if you just make a simple observation you will not feel emotion.

Let's consider a statement such as "Jake admires me." That's an assertion of fact only. By itself it does not spawn feelings. But if you add an evaluation, then you produce an emotion. For example: "I *like* Jake admiring me." "I *love* Jake admiring me." "I *dislike* Jake admiring me." "I *loathe* Jake admiring me."

The strength of any "like" exists on a scale from 0 percent to 99.9 percent. (You can never prefer something at the 100 percent level because no matter how strongly you desire it, theoretically you could always yearn for it even more.)

If you prefer to be admired by Jake only slightly (at the 10 percent level, say) you will feel mildly pleased that he's admiring you and mildly displeased should he despise you. If, on the other hand, you prefer it at the 90 percent level, you will feel rather great when Jake admires you and greatly disappointed if he doesn't. Thus preferences create emotions. Since the preferences are based on a scale from 0 percent to 99.9 percent, *appropriate* or reasonable emotions come from preferences.

On the other hand, inappropriate or unreasonable emotions come from demands rather than preferences. What we call "demands" consist of magical, absolutistic, moralistic notions, and take the form of "musts" and "shoulds." For example: "Jake absolutely MUST admire me and it would be awful if he doesn't!"

"Musts" and "shoulds" lead to dysfunctional emotions—emotions that eat away at you, such as anger, anxiety, depression, guilt, and self-pity. Demandingness also leads to self-defeating behaviors such as procrastination, violence, and addictions, including alcoholism, substance abuse, overeating, gambling, and compulsive shopping.

The key to the *Three Minute Therapy* method is that it's perfectly rational and generally helpful to have *preferences*, especially quite strong preferences, but it's irrational and harmful to turn these preferences into *demands* or "musts." The majority of emotional problems arise because individuals believe that something or other MUST be, or not be. For example: "I MUST do well at school" (instead of "I PREFER to do well at school"); "I MUST not feel anxious" (instead of "It's UNFORTUNATE that I some-

7

times feel anxious"); or "My spouse MUST not behave coldly toward me" (instead of "I find it UNPLEASANT when my spouse behaves coldly toward me").

Allied with the judgment that something must (or must not) happen is the judgment that when it doesn't (or does) happen, this is awful, terrible, horrible, shameful, or unbearable. In many different ways, we will show how these judgments lead to personal difficulties. Thinking in terms of "musts" is the essence of unrealistic, irrational thinking, as well as self-defeating behavior.

There are three kinds of "musts" or irrational demands. We will meet each one of these many times in the following chapters:

- "Must" #1, demands on oneself.

- "Must" #2, demands on other people.

- "Must" #3, demands on the situation (or on the Universe).

Many therapists try to persuade their clients to adopt only realistic goals and to give up unrealistic goals. But even unrealistic goals may be harmless, or perhaps beneficial, as long as they are viewed simply as preferences and not as demands.

Suppose you have an unrealistic goal, such as becoming the richest person alive. And you think, "I keenly PREFER to be the richest, and it's unfortunate that I'm not." And you want that at the 90 percent level—very, very much.

Most therapies would say: "Holding that kind of unrealistic goal will cause you emotional problems. Think more realistically. Don't compare yourself to others and just aim to do your best. Then you won't feel so pressured." But such advice is wrong and could be harmful.

It's wrong, because since you only have a preference, not a "must," you will not feel disturbed about not being the richest person alive. It could be harmful advice since high, lofty goals, no matter how unattainable—if viewed as preferences, not demands—motivate and add passion, challenge, and involvement to life. Great wonders have been accomplished by individuals striving for the impossible, and such striving doesn't necessarily make those individuals unhappy.

In writing this book, our serious ambition was to have a national best-seller. Although the chances of this are small, such an unrealistic aspiration has helped keep us absorbed and engaged in our writing in a concerted, goal-directed way.

## Disputing "Shoulds" and "Musts"

Merely pointing out to sufferers that their "musty," demanding thinking is responsible for their emotional problems will rarely dispel those problems, even if the sufferers agree. They will probably still fall into their old demanding thought patterns—unless they take a further step.

The most effective technique is for the sufferer to identify the specific "must" or irrational demand, which causes her problem, and then to *actively dispute* that "must." The person could write out an exercise each day in which the "musts" are listed and the reasons stated why they are groundless. Often, examination of a person's habitual judgments reveals that they are unwarranted demands, and looking closely at these judgments is all that it takes for the sufferer to see this. But sometimes it's necessary to argue persuasively with the sufferer.

This brings us to another distinctive feature of Three Minute Therapy. It involves arguing or debating. As a therapist, I debate with my clients, appealing to their reason to get them to look at their situation differently. Anyone using this book had better be prepared to debate with themselves. Many therapists refuse to argue or debate with clients, not recognizing that the client's own intelligent mind can play an active role in the cure.

It's important to dispute your "musts" *actively.* Anyone who has tried to grasp or memorize material in a hurry (such as a student before an exam), knows that merely reading through the material is not very effective. It's better to be actively engaged, for example by writing out the material. Then it's more likely to sink in.

## Three Minute Exercises

Throughout this book we will be giving Three Minute Exercises which follow an ABCDEF format. Let's see how these exercises work. Suppose you feel angry that Jake doesn't admire you:

A. (**A**ctivating event): Jake doesn't admire me.

B. (irrational **B**elief): Jake MUST admire me.

C. (emotional **C**onsequences): Anger.

As we have seen, it's the "must" that's making you angry, not just the lack of Jake's admiration. If instead of a "must" you had a *preference,* you would feel sensibly sorry and displeased, not foolishly angry and infuriated. Thus, the question becomes: "How do you eliminate the 'must' and thereby eradicate your anger?"

Answer: Proceed to "D." We set up a hypothesis, then look at the evidence for and against that hypothesis. By using the scientific method, we're merely employing a more systematic form of the commonsense method of trial and error. We do this as young children, who are always making guesses about the world—forming hypotheses—then modifying or abandoning these guesses as they get more information.

>    D. (**D**isputing or questioning the irrational belief): "What is the evidence Jake MUST admire me?" "What's the evidence for my MUST?" Or in our example, "Why MUST Jake admire me?"

The correct response often comes as a surprise. There's no evidence for this MUST, or for any MUST. No reason exists that Jake MUST do other than he does, however desirable I might find it if he did. So now you have moved to:

>    E. (**E**ffective new thinking): I prefer that Jake admire me, but I can survive quite well if he doesn't.

It's true that you find it unpleasant that Jake doesn't admire you, that you would like it better if he did admire you, and perhaps even that it's wrong of him not to admire you. But the universe is not so constructed that people always do what's right or what other people would prefer them to do. Therefore, it's unrealistic to expect that this be bound to occur, and unreasonable to demand that it MUST occur.

Furthermore, when people demand that something MUST occur, they tend to think that something terrible happens when it doesn't occur, that this is intolerable or the end of the universe. They express this with words like "awful," "horrible," "appalling," or "dreadful." But the plain truth is that, although you don't like that Jake doesn't admire you, you can survive quite well without Jake's admiring you.

Having replaced your "B" (your irrational demand that Jake MUST admire you) with "E" (your reasonable preference that Jake admire you) you will then begin to experience:

> F. (new **F**eeling): regret or disappointment, but no anger.

## *Practice, Repetition, Reinforcement*

A common way to begin learning to swim is to first rehearse the correct strokes on land. That's a useful preparation, but you will never become a competent swimmer by that method alone; you'll just thrash about awkwardly in the water. When the correct habits have become ingrained, after much practice on land and in the water, then you can call yourself a swimmer.

It's the same when learning a language—Italian, for instance. At first you speak Italian mechanically and haltingly. You don't expect to speak fluent Italian after one lesson. You keep practicing and increasing your skill—programming your brain and body with the correct habits. After you become thoroughly familiar with Italian, you feel it and live it. Italian becomes "second nature" to you. The stages you go through in order to think straight and feel good are comparable to the stages of learning swimming or Italian. At first you make an effort to perceive that your "musts" are irrational, illogical, and self-defeating. Later you will deeply believe and feel this to be true.

The way to improve is simple and clear-cut but not easy: practice, practice, practice. Continuous and meaningful practice is required. More is better.

As with swimming or Italian, once you've acquired the skill and really feel it and believe it, you're not finished with the discipline. You're sure to get rusty and experience setbacks if you don't continue your reinforcement.

Compare this with brushing your teeth. Suppose you brush and floss your teeth conscientiously twice a day for a year and then visit the dentist and she exclaims: "No cavities!"

Do you abandon brushing your teeth? Clearly not. You know full well that if you do, the plaque and bacteria will slowly creep back in and start their dirty work. That's because humans naturally and effortlessly manufacture plaque and bacteria as a never-ending process.

It's the same with your "musts." As a human, you're a "must"- and "should"-creating animal. You find it easy to take those preferences that rate as important to you and make "musts" out of them. It's in your genes as well as in your upbringing. You don't have to be taught either to build plaque or to invent "musts." True, you can make the plaque build-up worse by eating junk food, and you can make the "must" build-up worse by practicing and reinforcing your "musty" thoughts. On the other hand, you can halt and reverse the build-up of plaque or "musts" by brushing and flossing, or disputing and questioning, regularly.

Similarly, your facility in speaking English would start deteriorating should you move to Italy and speak Italian exclusively. Even with your native tongue, a lack of practice will make you rusty. If you don't wish to get rusty, keep practicing.

If you just read this book through and nod your head in agreement, you may find it entertaining, and it will probably give you some slight help. But that is *not* applying the method of *Three Minute Therapy*. The big returns will come only from applying the exercises to your own problems, such as writing out the exercises, and perhaps then reading them into your phone and listening to it frequently.

When you learn the basics of Three Minute Therapy, it may not immediately translate into feeling and acting significantly better. But as you conscientiously practice, you'll progress to a higher level of skill and the rewards will come. Three Minute Therapy will then become a tool for you to quickly think yourself out of emotional pain and turmoil.

People often come to therapy believing that they can be finally and permanently "cured," with no further work required on their part. For most, this is not realistic. People are naturally inclined to irrational, demanding thinking, and it's advisable to combat this inclination by performing the exercises indefinitely, just as it is advisable to keep on brushing your teeth. Once the basic understanding has been gained, future analysis and correction of faulty thinking will usually require no more than three minutes as the occasion arises.

# 2

## *Worry: Sharks in the Swimming Pool*

*My life has been full of terrible misfortunes, most of which never happened.*
—MICHEL EYQUEM DE MONTAIGNE (1533–1592)

Chris was an ambitious computer consultant haunted by a peculiar anxiety—his fear that nuts and bolts, or other components of airplanes, would fall on his head, possibly killing him. If he heard the sound of an aircraft while walking outside, he would consider taking shelter. He felt anxious even if the plane were not directly overhead—for he speculated that falling objects might travel some lateral distance if they were thrown to the side by the airplane turning or by a powerful wind.

This is one of a long list of some of my clients' farfetched fears. Here are a few other examples:

- A 38-year-old elevator inspector was obsessed with the thought that he might suddenly decide to become a woman and have a sex-change operation—though he never had felt such a desire, and in his sexual preferences and behavior he was an entirely typical heterosexual male.

- A lawyer was afraid that she might inadvertently impregnate herself, by touching microscopic deposits of semen on objects, such as a doorknob, and then accidentally touching herself while in the bathroom.

- A middle-aged, married accountant who had sent an angry but non-threatening memo to a former boss, began to worry that the boss might sue her, causing her to lose her house and all her savings and become a bag lady.

- A timid lady, who would never hurt a fly, always avoided listening to news broadcasts and became panicky if she overheard part of such a broadcast, because she was afraid that she might hear of some atrocity such as a mass killing and be uncontrollably impelled to copy it.

- A young music teacher was afraid to go into a public swimming pool in a Midwestern city because there might be sharks there, which might eat him, or at the very least bite off one of his feet. An intelligent person, he readily admitted that sharks did not regularly inhabit swimming pools. He knew that it would be difficult to smuggle a live shark into such a pool; that if there were a shark there, he ought to be able to see it; and that any self-respecting shark would no doubt be so bothered by the chlorine it would not lie quietly in wait at the bottom of the pool. Nonetheless, he described himself as petrified by the thought that such a thing might happen, so that he had given up his twice-weekly swim. For my part, I conceded that I could not conclusively prove that he would never meet a shark in a swimming pool!

Such absurd fears are more common than many of us realize. There is, for instance, a cult magazine titled *Shark Fear*, and legends about sharks, piranhas, or alligators in the plumbing are rife from Florida to New York

City. And although these fears may sound ridiculous to most people, that is no consolation to the individuals who suffer from them.

Here are some other fears which are *widely* held—I have encountered them all many times—and which cause real pain to millions of people. Consider whether they are any more reasonable than the preposterous fears mentioned above:

- The fear of being on a high floor of a tall building because one side of the building might abruptly crumble, or you might suddenly feel an irresistible urge to jump through the window.

- The fear that one will be possessed by an unconquerable urge to do something outrageous and embarrassing in public. For instance, someone sitting in the audience of a theater may suddenly be struck by the thought that he might get up from his seat, rush to the front, and jump onto the stage with the actors. He may then sit there in a cold sweat, not enjoying the play, because of his worry that he may at any moment uncontrollably do this outrageous thing that he does not in the least want to do.

- The fear that one will die while asleep. Someone may notice that his heartbeat slows down as he becomes drowsy, and he may then start worrying that it will stop altogether if he falls asleep.

- The fear of killing or mutilating someone close to you. Mothers sometimes experience a panicky fear that they will plunge a knife into their child, and husbands sometimes torment themselves with the fear that they will strangle their wives.

These commonplace anxieties are just as unreasonable as the more unusual ones mentioned earlier. We can easily see that they are all fears of something extremely unlikely. This gives a clue to the root of much unnecessary anxiety: a demand that one gets an iron-clad, sure-fire, one-hundred-percent *guarantee* that something unpleasant *absolutely will not* occur.

With unlikely events, people are more influenced by a possibility that catches their imagination in some dramatic, spectacular way, rather than by the objective likelihood that it will occur. For instance, you often hear people argue against moving to California because they might die in an earthquake, whereas the death toll from cold weather—not to mention tornados and thunderstorms—east of the Rockies hugely exceeds fatalities from earthquakes in the West. Or some people will be nervous about flying because of the possibility of a fatal plane crash, but driving to the airport is objectively more dangerous.

## Is This Blood That I See Before Me?

It was a blustery, overcast autumn day. At 11:55 A.M., Jerzy rushed out of his office and dashed to his regular restaurant. When he arrived, he was relieved to see that he had indeed got there ahead of the long line that formed every day around noon. He settled into his usual seat at a corner table, began to read his newspaper, and absentmindedly ordered his lunch. When the meal arrived, he picked up his fork—and froze.

Jerzy had spotted something amid the green of the broccoli and the orange of the yams—a tiny spot of crimson. "What if it's blood?" he thought. "And what if it's HIV-positive?" Jerzy was seized by the thought that he might get AIDS. He fled the restaurant, leaving his plate untouched, and wouldn't go back.

In the weeks that followed, Jerzy spent much time worrying about the possibility that he might catch AIDS and began to lose sleep. He stopped eating out alone, and when eating out with close friends, he would ask them to inspect his food and reassure him that there was no blood on it.

It is, of course, millions of times more likely that you will die from food poisoning following a restaurant meal than that you will pick up AIDS that way. But Jerzy never gave a thought to that less sensational, more prosaic possibility.

## *A Dread of Uncertainty*

To some extent, Jerzy's anxiety resulted from his telling himself, "I MUST not get AIDS." However, the main anxiety trigger consisted of his demand for *certainty*: "Since there is a one-in-a-billion chance that I could contract AIDS when dining out, the fates MUST guarantee me a *zero*-in-a-billion chance."

Demanding certainty in an uncertain universe leads, paradoxically, to concluding that *unlikely* dangers are virtually guaranteed to happen. And if you insist on absolute, one-hundred-percent security, you create emotional insecurity for yourself.

For example, the fear of flying often stems from the idea: "I MUST have a guarantee, signed and sealed by the fates, that the plane won't crash." Consequently, once someone who fears flying agonizingly drags himself aboard the plane, whenever there's the slightest turbulence, or the flight attendant frowns, the individual is convinced: "This is it! The plane's going down!"

"Cowards die many times before their deaths," says Shakespeare's Julius Caesar. More generally, it's true that habitual worriers suffer a thousand times more agonies than they would if they stopped worrying about remote possibilities.

## *Jerzy's Three Minute Exercise*

So it was with Jerzy and his worry about AIDS. He demanded guaranteed immunity, and thus saw AIDS everywhere. We targeted his "need" for certainty in Three Minute Exercises such as this one:

A. (**A**ctivating event): I'm dining out and I see something red in my food. What if it's AIDS-infected?

B. (irrational **B**elief): Life MUST give me an iron-clad guarantee that I will not get AIDS by eating this food.

C. (emotional **C**onsequences): Anxiety.

D. (**D**isputing): What is the evidence that life MUST give me an ironclad guarantee that I will not contract AIDS while eating out?

E. (**E**ffective new thinking): It would be lovely if I could get guarantees in life, but none exist. Certainty is a figment of my imagination, and besides, I don't HAVE TO be absolutely certain of anything. The probability is high that I will never contract AIDS. There are (probably) only probabilities, and I can live happily with them as long as I refuse to demand more. Oh yes, if there were any certainty (which there isn't), it would be the certainty that as long as I insist on

20

guarantees, I'm doomed to keep making myself anxious. It's a nuisance not knowing for sure that I won't contract AIDS, but no evidence demonstrates that life MUST not give me such inconvenience. Life has much uncertainty. Too bad! It's never the doubt itself, but rather my "awfulizing" about it, that worries me.

F. (new **F**eeling): Concern, rather than anxiety, about eating out.

## Tony's Worries

Tony, 25, was tall and thin with curly dark hair and an olive complexion. His problem was escalating, yet he joked wryly about it, giving me a variant of a standard witticism I have heard from dozens of clients: "After years of false starts and immature attempts," he announced, with mock seriousness, "I've now completely mastered the art of worrying!"

Tony had spent six months in traditional therapy. "It helped me understand myself better, or so I naively supposed at the time. I tried to ignore the fact that the whole time I was getting worse." He terminated therapy when it came to him one day that he could end up single-handedly putting his psychoanalyst's kid through college. When Tony's girlfriend landed a job with a prestigious law firm in San Francisco, they left New York. Now Tony felt it was again time to face his problem, so he returned to therapy.

Tony gave me a brief history of his worries:

"I can remember worrying about making errors when I was on the Little League baseball team. And then worrying when I was in high school, before a test and during a test—and, come to think of it, until I got my grade.

"I always thought that I worried more than almost everyone, worried about sillier things, and dealt with worrying worse than most people. I even worried about the fact that I was such a worrier."

Tony was employed as a bank loan officer, a job he considered stressful. Every morning, the day ahead loomed like an ordeal about to unfold.

"When I start a new project at work, tackle a difficult problem, or when I have a ton of work to do, I worry. And I worry about learning new skills and about doing so poorly that I would lose my job. Overall, it gets more stressful as I move up the corporate ladder.

"There are times work isn't so bad, like when I have something that's not too challenging, or don't have time pressure. But generally, my worrying leads me to dislike my job. Sometimes I'm up all night worrying, and then I'm tired the next day and waste time daydreaming at work. I have concentration difficulties. When I do sleep, I sleep poorly. I do badly at work because of my worrying."

## *Job Security Worries*

"The root of your problem, Tony," I suggested, "doesn't lie in your Little League experiences, nor in your promotions at work, nor in your shaky financial situation should you lose your job. Rather, it lies in your demandingness—your 'musts,' your 'have to's,' your 'got to's' about your goals."

I explained to Tony how "musty" thinking generates anxiety. I described the three types of demands: demands on oneself, demands on others, and demands on the universe.

"It's clear to me what your major 'musts' are. Would you care to hazard a guess?" "Let's see, probably must number three: a demand on my situation—a demand on the universe. 'Concentrating MUST not be so difficult,' 'Sleep SHOULD come easily,' 'My job MUST last forever'?"

"Exactly! And why MUST your job last forever?"

"Because if I lose my job, I'm royally screwed. I'll never get such a good job. I've worked my way up. I'll have to start all over again, at square one!"

Notice that Tony's fear that he would lose his job was not a "silly fear" like the ones that started this chapter. Employees at all levels, even dependable, hardworking employees, do sometimes lose their jobs. But when asked why this was terrible, Tony responded in exaggerated, melodramatic terms about the consequences of losing his job.

"Let's suppose that this is the case—although it's unlikely—that you'd be starting at square one, even with your experience. We could certainly list fifteen or twenty disadvantages of your getting fired. But since everyone faces setbacks in life, why MUST you not?"

"When you put it that way, I admit that it wouldn't be the end of the world if I lost my job. It would be unwelcome, but not a calamity. I suppose I'd better join the human race and face the sad fact that I could experience setbacks in my life, just like everyone else."

To reinforce this, Tony and I made a list of the reasons why his belief that his job MUST last forever is false. Here's what he wrote:

**Reasons why "My job MUST last forever" is false:**

1. If I lose my job, I lose it! Reality is reality, not the way I think it has "got to" be.

23

2. Although I keenly prefer not to lose my job, a preference does not equal a "got to."

3. Although I would have extra financial and employment hassles if I lost my job, that's all I would have—hassles, not horrors.

4. It could be nice to have a respite from work, which would provide a longed-for break to visit my brother in Italy.

5. I have savings I could live on for a while. I would be able to take my time and do a really excellent job of finding the best job available.

6. Losing my job could give me just the push that I have been lacking to take a chance on my dream—starting my own business as a computer consultant.

7. Losing my job would give me a golden opportunity to practice accepting misfortunes, rather than needlessly worrying about them.

8. I would see, concretely, that even the worst-case scenario is not as bad as I had anticipated.

9. If I lose my job, this would be a bad situation, but it would not make me a bad or worthless person.

10. I could be more money-conscious, for example, move into a smaller apartment, eat at home more, and buy a new car in five years rather than immediately. This would mean some deprivation, but I've survived deprivation before, and I will survive it in the future.

11. The simple fact of losing my job, by itself, can never disturb me. Only my bellyaching about it can do that.

12. Even if I never get a job as well-paying as my current one, I could accept that and still considerably enjoy life, although I could enjoy it even more with a better salary.

13. Losing my job would provide an opportunity to eventually get a position that may have certain advantages over this one: a more supportive boss, more friendly co-workers, less pressure, more interesting work, shorter commute times, less crowded work space, or better pay.

14. Pressuring myself not to get fired will not help me keep my job. Moreover, it could turn into a self-fulfilling prophecy: the more I demand this, the more stressed and distracted I get, and the worse I perform.

15. In the larger sense, all jobs are temporary. Career changes, unemployment, and lost jobs are part of life.

16. If I start at "square one" at a new job, I could work my way up the ladder as I've done before.

17. Everyone has significant discomforts, inconveniences, and hassles in life. This is part of the human condition. No reason exists why I have "got to" be exempt.

18. It could actually be a relief not to be so focused on getting promotions and moving up the corporate ladder.

Tony read this list into his phone. He listened to it at home and in his car. He found this daily reinforcement surprisingly effective in eroding his "got to's" and thereby drastically reducing his anxiety.

## *Anxiety, Fear, and Worry*

Fear and anxiety are basically the same emotion. We use these two words in subtly different ways. We are more likely to call the emotion "anxiety" if the thing feared seems vague or uncertain, but it's the same animal.

Worry is the practice of anxiously pondering something, usually repeatedly and at length. So, if you feel a twinge of panic when called upon to make a speech, that's anxiety, but not worry. If, on the other hand, you keep anxiously thinking about the speech you are scheduled to make next week, that's both anxiety *and* worry.

Worry is anxious pondering; worry is a package made up of both pondering and anxiety. Or, in the form of an equation:

$$Worry = Pondering + Anxiety$$

Popular fallacies about worry mostly arise because people do not distinguish between pure pondering without anxiety and pondering with added anxiety. People may say, "Don't worry about that," when what they really mean is, "Don't concern yourself with that; don't give it another thought." This way of speaking is in itself harmless, of course, but mistakes arise when people believe that thinking hard about a problem has to be an anxious experience.

A chess grandmaster may spend hours pondering a position, trying to find the best move, but there is no reason why he need feel anxious about it, and he is more likely to analyze the position better if he is free of anxiety. The same applies to Proust writing a great novel or Beethoven writing one of his symphonies.

People will often say that worry is useless, and that it's best to stop worrying, by which they usually mean, stop thinking about the problem. However, pondering some problem may not be useless—one may come up with an idea that would solve or alleviate it.

If you have an important interview tomorrow, you may worry about it, that is think anxiously about it. And this *may* do you some good in the interview—research shows that people do better on such occasions if they re-hearse them in their minds beforehand. Yet the good that comes from such worrying comes despite the anxiety, not because of it. Merely thinking about the interview, without feeling anxious about it, will do just as much good and probably more. People who think anxiously about such things usually think far less efficiently than those who think non-anxiously.

Contrary to the usual view, it's possible to feel *keenly concerned* about something without feeling in the least *anxious* about it. Ted and Timothy are great buddies and have a vigorous, friendly rivalry at table tennis, which gives them much enjoyment. They are each keenly deter-mined to win, and excited and exhilarated whether they win or lose, though also distinctly disappointed if they lose. There is no *anxiety* in their concern to win. They don't *fear* losing, though they decidedly prefer not to lose.

This kind of example refutes the popular but mis-taken view that *some* anxiety is helpful because we need adrenaline to give us extra speed or concentration in mo-ments of crisis. Extra adrenaline can be helpful in some sit-uations, but we can have the extra adrenaline without any fear or anxiety, as Ted and Timothy do during table tennis, or as people often do during sex.

True, worriers do often spend a lot of time thinking uselessly about their problems, their thoughts going round and round in a repeating groove to no effect. But if they would learn to think about their problems without anxiety, they would then spontaneously stop thinking excessively about those problems where further thought was obviously pointless.

How can we learn to think about problems without anxiety? The anxiety—the fear—always comes from our demands, our "musts." The way you can stop worrying and yet continue to think hard about a problem is to challenge and uproot your "musts." When you find yourself worrying about some situation, it's not the situation, by itself, that is generating your anxiety. It's your "musts" that make you anxious, and tackling your "musts" is the best way to reduce your anxiety.

# 3

# Self-Esteem: The "Feel Good About Yourself" Trap

*A man is a kind of inverted thermometer, the bulb uppermost, and the column of self-valuation is all the time going up and down.*
—OLIVER WENDELL HOLMES, SR. (1809–1894)

At age 25, Jerry was tall and good-looking, with a broad-shouldered, athletic build. He was an expert surfer and water-skier. His Valentino suit hadn't left him much change out of $6,000. He drove a BMW to work and a Porsche to the beach. Unlike some upwardly mobile achievers, Jerry had a polite and unassuming manner, and with his warm, contagious smile, he communicated instant likeability. He had recently become engaged to an intelligent and beautiful law student.

Jerry felt good about himself. He awoke each morning eager to face the challenges of the day and took pleasure in the exercise of his own abilities. He successfully managed his own, rapidly-expanding real estate business, and was proud of his accomplishments. He undoubtedly possessed what is often called "high self-esteem."

No one who knew Jerry suspected that he was an emotional time bomb, ticking away.

## The Winner Becomes a Loser

Six months later, when Jerry came to see me, he was miserable and preoccupied with suicide. For the past month, he had been waking up at 4:00 A.M., with a knot in his stomach. He then felt anxious for the rest of the day and was often depressed. In his relations with his fiancée, he was experiencing erection problems and had begun to brood about becoming permanently impotent, a prospect he perceived as horribly shameful.

"I'm terrified that I'm going to lose everything, including my mind. I can't sleep. Nothing is fun anymore. I cry every morning before leaving for work. I'm beside myself and I don't know what to do. I'm at the end of my rope."

## The Problem Separation Technique

Whenever someone is suffering emotionally, as Jerry was, I have found that a simple procedure usually clarifies the situation:

- First, identify the Practical Problem.

- Second, identify the Emotional Problem.

- Third, get the sufferer to look at the connection between his Emotional Problem and his Practical Problem.

I explained to Jerry the difference between a Practical and an Emotional Problem: "It seems to me," I told him, "that your Practical Problem involves the success of your business. How can you start making money in real estate again? Or would you do better to change your line of work?

"The Emotional Problem is that you're upsetting yourself about your current setbacks. Why not do your best with the real estate, without ripping yourself up inside about it?"

"I wish I could. But I'd feel I wasn't good enough, like a failure, if my business went down the drain. Todd just made a two million dollar sale—he picked up an unbelievable commission with that one. I'm just nowhere in comparison."

I nearly always find that a person comes to me convinced that his Practical Problem automatically generates his Emotional Problem. My first job is to undermine this conviction, showing him that he causes his Emotional Problem by the way he thinks. His Practical Problem is defined by his preferences, but his Emotional Problem springs from his "musts." Then, the Practical and Emotional Problems can be tackled separately.

This may not sound like great progress, but it really is. Once the person begins to seriously tackle the Emotional Problem separately from the Practical Problem, there is often a prompt improvement in the Practical Problem.

## The Self-Rating Roller-Coaster

Without realizing it, Jerry had become caught in the "feel good about yourself" trap. When he was making lots of sales, he rated himself as a pretty fine person, and this gave him high self-esteem.

His mistake was not that he liked being successful. His mistake was that he rated himself highly—as a total person—because of his success. As a result, when he became less successful, he automatically gave himself a lower rating and began to feel miserable.

As I probed, Jerry admitted more and more clearly that he believed himself to be totally unworthy. Like many people in this frame of mind, Jerry believed that his own strong feeling that he was unworthy was somehow evidence that he was unworthy. This kind of reasoning reinforces itself in an endless circle: the more worthless he felt, the more "evidence" he had to prove he was indeed worthless!

I asked Jerry: "Assuming that your performance in real estate is inferior right now, how does this make you totally inferior? After all, you are an imperfect human, like everyone else, so it's to be expected that you will sometimes act imperfectly. How does this prove that you're worthless?"

"I don't know," he replied. "I can't prove it. All I know is that I feel worthless, so I must be worthless."

Now, of course, it's easy for an outsider, someone not involved in Jerry's life, to see that Jerry is being unreasonable. It's obvious that there's something irrational in this dogmatic insistence that he is an inferior worm. But it's just as irrational for someone to maintain that they're a great person because things are going well for them.

Psychotherapists who preach "high self-esteem" overlook this logical connection. They encounter miserable people and observe that these people frequently have a very low opinion of themselves. These "Dr. Feelgood" therapists then conclude that the appropriate treatment is to encourage their clients to give themselves a higher self-rating. But self-rating—any self-rating, high or low—is often the root of the problem.

## **Deluded Dunces and Self-Satisfied Psychopaths**

Trying to improve people's rating of themselves runs into numerous problems. One of the more pathetic of these arises when people who, objectively considered, perform poorly at some specific task are encouraged to view themselves as outstandingly good, and information about their poor performance is downplayed.

In a recent study, 13-year-olds in six countries (the U.S., Britain, Canada, Ireland, Korea, and Spain) were given a standardized math test. In addition, they were asked to rate the statement: "I am good at mathematics."

The Americans judged their abilities the most highly (68 percent agreed with the statement!). But on the actual math test the Americans came last.

Some educators think that these two results were related. These poor to average students, who felt buoyed by the fantasy that they were superbly competent, were victims of the "self-esteem curriculum," designed to make the kids feel good about themselves no matter what.

High self-esteem can involve self-delusion. It's not true that people who feel good about themselves always perform better. It's a cruel deception to convey the impression that success comes easily if you have a "positive" attitude. Performing well is in fact closely related to High Frustration Tolerance—the ability to cope serenely with difficulties and setbacks. Outstanding accomplishments usually require immense dedication, continuous, painful investment of arduous effort over a long period of time. They also require some inborn talent, which is not equally distributed.

It may be comparatively harmless for some people to go through life under the delusion that they're good at something when in fact they are not. However, if they derive self-esteem from this fantasy, they may be set up for a shattering disappointment if ever they decide to face reality.

This isn't the only problem arising from high self-esteem. Many theorists have supposed that violent criminals suffer from low self-esteem and can be rehabilitated by having their self-esteem raised. But a careful review of the evidence by three psychologists (Roy Baumeister, Joseph Boden, and Laura Smart) found that most violent people think very highly of themselves; their unrealistically high self-evaluations predispose them to be violent. As these authors point out, treating rapists, spouse batterers, or murderers by trying to convince them that they are superior beings is pointless, since this is what such people already believe.

## Your Successes Aren't You—Your Failures Aren't You

Jerry had difficulty seeing my point. "What was wrong with feeling so good about being successful? Wouldn't I be better off if I could get back to the way I felt six months ago?"

"Well, that option isn't available," I pointed out. "If you could snap your fingers and start making money again, you would do so. There's nothing wrong with feeling good about being successful. What creates problems is to rate yourself highly when you are successful, and to feel good only because you have given yourself a high rating. It would be better never to rate your self, merely rate your specific behavior."

"That seems to make sense," he conceded. "But it's not the way I think."

"But what does your thinking accomplish?"

"Well, when I was successful, feeling pretty great."

"Feeling great about your self. But you can still feel happy and content by feeling great about your accomplishments, without dragging your total self into it. And then you wouldn't set yourself up for feeling like a worm when the real estate market crashes."

"Hmm. Very interesting. So it's unwise to put myself up on a pedestal or, on the other hand, look down on myself. You know, I feel a little less depressed already, just viewing it from that perspective. It's very different from how I'm used to thinking."

## Jerry's Three Minute Exercise

Jerry was beginning to get the message. I explained the method of written Three Minute Exercises, which he began to practice every day. Here is a typical one:

A. (**A**ctivating event): My business is losing money.

B. (irrational **B**elief): I MUST be making money or else I'm no good.

C. (emotional **C**onsequences): Depression.

D. (**D**isputing): Why MUST I make a lot of money? How does it make me no good if I don't have a high income?

E. (**E**ffective new thinking): No law of the universe states that I MUST make a lot of money. Reality is reality, independent of my views about it, so I may as well fully accept the vicissitudes of the real estate market, along with my own imperfections. I don't magically turn into a worm even if I lose all my money. It's not my disappointing income, but my own self-downing about it, that makes me feel depressed. Likewise, it's not the success itself, but rather my view of it, that makes me feel like a wonderful person. Success does not change my essence and make me "good," just as failure doesn't change me into a wretched no-good. My goal in life is to enjoy myself, not to prove myself.

F.  (new **F**eeling): Concern and steady determination rather than intense anxiety or depression.

## A Self-Defeating Syllogism

Jerry's case is a striking one in that he had changed, inside a few months, from high self-esteem to low self-esteem. But Jerry's thinking is commonplace:

1.  I WANT TO FEEL GOOD. (Nothing wrong with this!)

2.  To feel good, I have to feel good about myself. (But this is a blunder.)

3.  Feeling good about myself means thinking that I am a worthy person.

4.  I can prove to myself that I'm a worthy person by doing well at x (making money, passing my exams, keeping fit, attracting members of the opposite sex, being good in bed, keeping my family happy).

5.  Oops! I've done badly at x. So now I'm worthless. I FEEL BAD.

## *Your Income Isn't You*

Jerry's problem also illustrates a highly popular but erroneous belief—the belief that our money income measures our worth or our success in life. This false belief is a source of anxiety and depression to millions.

Our money income represents only what other people choose to pay for the services we choose to supply them. It's not a judgment on our "souls" or on our dignity as human beings. There's nothing demeaning or insulting in having a low income. It's not even a final judgment on our abilities—Mozart died poor.

If we can increase our money income, then we can afford more goods and services, enabling us to accomplish our aims more completely and perhaps to lead a fuller life. That's wonderful, but we may value our free time or our avoidance of pressures too highly to do what's required to raise our income beyond a certain point. In that case, it would be a foolish mistake to suppose that we have to pursue a higher money income as an end in itself.

## *Running Into Trouble*

Ned was a 46-year-old successful veterinarian with his own animal hospital. He consulted me for help with his marital discord, but toward the end of our first session, the discussion took a different tack.

"I may have discovered a way to feel better—to escape my usual depression—when my wife berates me or nags me," he volunteered, unexpectedly.

"How's that?" I queried.

"By running," Ned responded. "I used to jog once in a while, but lately I've taken up running more seriously. I consistently jog at least five miles a day, and I've started running competitively. So now, when Kristan bugs me, I can ignore her. Running makes me feel better about myself, instead of down in the dumps from being nagged by Kristan. I feel proud that I can discipline myself, and after a long, hard run or a good race, I feel really elated."

"So you consider yourself a better person for becoming self-disciplined and getting yourself in such terrific shape. And you think that if Kristan can't appreciate you, that's her tough luck!"

"Exactly!"

"But this is adding to your problem!"

"Problem?" Ned was taken aback. "At least I haven't felt so rotten lately. Isn't that improving upon my problem?"

"No. An alcoholic may feel better after a drink, but the drink doesn't necessarily improve his problem. You may in fact be making the problem worse." Since Ned was still somewhat baffled, I explained that he started out delighted at his newfound self-discipline and running ability. That delight was altogether appropriate. But then he mistakenly rated his total self as good because of his running. He was manufacturing and nurturing his elation by judging his whole self in terms of a few of his behaviors.

"All right," he said. "So I've been rating my total self in terms of my running. So I've been elated and I've been pleased by my elation. I still don't see how that hurts me."

"It hurts you because it sets you up to feel hurt or depressed. You don't realize that it works as a double-edged sword."

"No, I guess I don't."

"Well, when you run well you feel elated. But when you run or race badly, or Kristan criticizes you, you get depressed."

"That's right. I do get depressed then!"

"But as long as you insist on rating yourself, you're turning yourself into an emotional yo-yo, at the mercy of your latest performance."

"I think I see. I put myself 'up' when I run well and consistently. But then I'm all the more inclined to put myself 'down' when things go badly."

## *Self-Raters Are Born but Can Be Unmade*

We're all like Ned: we are born and raised to rate ourselves. Understandably, we have difficulty thinking in any other way. But there's an alternative. You can analyze how well you do without rating your total self. You can accept yourself no matter what—whether you do well, poorly, or don't do anything at all. You are never forced to judge yourself as great or as unworthy—to put yourself up or down.

Self-rating is unnecessary, and it causes serious emotional and practical problems:

1. If you insist on rating yourself, your thinking becomes self-centered instead of problem-centered. If you don't rate yourself but acknowledge there is a problem, it becomes easier to analyze that problem, and an agreeable solution may be found. Considering yourself a "hopeless loser" or a "disgusting worm" is not a problem that can be analyzed and tackled. It is a conviction that points in only one direction: endless preoccupation with what a hopeless loser or disgusting worm you are! This is simply not helpful. It doesn't prompt any constructive action.

2. If you rate yourself as good or bad, you tend to suppose that this is your unchanging essence, that if you did badly yesterday, you're likely to do badly today or tomorrow. You tend to become frozen in your own self-rating. Everyone has a great many good and bad traits; we're all imperfect yet capable of improvement. But self-rating causes us to fasten on a few traits and then make an over-simple judgment about ourselves.

3. A low self-rating makes you feel miserable, and a high self-rating sets you up for a poor self-rating whenever things go wrong. High and low self-ratings are not symmetrical—there's an inherent tendency for self-raters to move toward a low self-rating. Most human intentions don't work out quite as planned, and there's a natural tendency to focus on disappointments and shortcomings.

4. Self-rating leads you to compare yourself pointlessly to other people. Feelings of superiority and inferiority then get in the way of pursuing your aims.

## *If You Rate Yourself, You'll Berate Yourself*

We all know people who continually criticize themselves—the attractive woman who continually apologizes for her imperfect appearance, or the man who comments about his own unreliability or lack of achievement. Part of the intention of making such remarks is to admit your faults to other people so that they won't criticize you or will award you points for humility. But, in practice, issuing these public confessions:

- Is often found irritating by other people

- Usually doesn't persuade other people that you're a better person

- Needlessly draws their attention to faults of yours which they might overlook; and most importantly of all

- Tends to reinforce your own picture of yourself as unworthy

This verbal "self-downing" is an obvious manifestation of low self-esteem. It's natural to suppose that it can be fought by techniques for "raising self-esteem." But the best solution does not lie in learning how to squelch self-criticism or in practicing self-praise. While this may occasionally be useful, generally, raising self-esteem is counterproductive. It's better to uproot any amount of self-esteem—low or high. In other words, to stop self-rating.

## *Secondhand Self-Esteem*

Frequently a person's craving for self-esteem is linked to the approval of another person, often a spouse or parent. Tara, a strikingly attractive 41-year-old, was an executive secretary for a Madison Avenue advertising firm. She had a daughter in high school and a son in elementary school. She was tall, thin, and might have been taken for a model. Although she mentioned that she enjoyed going out with her husband and another couple on Saturday nights, she mostly just read me a litany of problems and gloomy feelings.

"I get nervous about everything and then I get depressed. I worry about illness and also I worry about work situations. I'm eaten up with envy for other people who have certain things better than I do. I hate meeting new people. I cry easily at movies and weddings, and always hate myself for crying. I constantly wish I were someone else. I feel like a weakling. I just despise the way I look. I can't relax, and I feel intimidated by my boss."

The tone of Tara's voice suggested that she was giving herself a good scolding, which she seemed ready to continue at some length.

"Sounds like a lot to deal with," I interrupted. "Out of all that, what seems to bother you the most these days?"

"Hard to say. I guess it's putting up with my mother when she comes to stay with us. She's very critical, and it's usually directed at me. Like last night, she was complaining that the house was a mess. I know I could do a better job at keeping the house clean, but I just can't find the time. My mother never went out to work, so she had all the time she needed to keep a spotless home. But somehow I feel that she's right: I really should keep the house neat and clean. I'm always uncomfortable in a messy house."

"Let's assume, as you claim, that your house is a holy mess."

"That's easy."

"And you're depressed about it."

"Yes, I am."

"This means you have a MUST in there somewhere."

"You mean like 'I MUST have a clean house'?"

"Exactly!"

"I do put myself down when I see dust or papers around the house," Tara confessed. "I do feel crummy about myself."

"But assuming the worst, that you really are a slovenly housekeeper, that's only one of many things in your life. So it doesn't follow that you, as a total person, are no good."

"But I'm not good at anything. I'm a lousy mother, my kids are not as personable as Marita's kids, and I'm always making faux pas at work and putting my foot in my mouth."

"But even if that's all true—and I suspect you're being perfectionistic in your self-judgments—you still have the potential to change. And your potential is an aspect of you. If you actualize your potential and improve in some of these areas, then we'll have additional things you're good at. Furthermore, in the future you might discover endeavors you never tried before that you find you have some talent for."

I pointed out to Tara another reason that making mistakes does not prove she is completely rotten. Just that she has succeeded at keeping herself alive, not gotten killed in a car accident, poisoned herself, or walked in front of a truck, proves that she doesn't always and only make mistakes or perform badly.

Some of Tara's "musts" were:

- I MUST have my mother approve of my house-keeping or else I'm worthless.

- I HAVE TO get all my cleaning done or else I turn into a worm.

- I SHOULD keep my house looking better than it does, otherwise I'm a lesser person.

- I have GOT TO do it immediately, or it proves I'm a total failure.

After disputing her "musts," Tara replaced them with these conclusions:

- Although my mother's approval is PREFERABLE, I can fully accept myself with her criticism.

- I WOULD LIKE to get all my cleaning done, but if I don't it mainly shows that I'm just an imperfect person acting imperfectly.

- I WISH my house looked better, but a less neat house doesn't mean I'm less of a total person.

- I PREFER to shape up my house right now and at worst I've failed in the housecleaning, but that failure does not measure my total essence.

## Tara's Three Minute Exercise

Tara quickly saw the point, and we soon began working on Three Minute Exercises. Here's one that she found particularly helpful.

A. (**A**ctivating event): My mother criticizes me and says the house looks as if I hadn't cleaned for a month when, in fact, I cleaned yesterday.

B. (irrational **B**elief): I MUST keep a spotlessly clean house and avoid my mother's criticism, or else I'm no good!

C. (emotional **C**onsequences): Hurt and depression.

D. (**D**isputing): What's the evidence I MUST keep a spotlessly clean house and avoid my mother's criticism or become no good?

E. (**E**ffective new thinking): Although I strongly prefer to keep a spotless house, I can find no reason why I MUST. Being an imperfect human, I will act imperfectly in many ways, so it's understandable that I may not have a perfectly clean house.

And if my mother thinks I'm no good, that's sad, but that's her opinion and doesn't magically turn me into a worm. I'm still me, not what she thinks is me. My mother isn't perfect either—nobody is. I'm never less of a person no matter how badly I do and no matter who disapproves of me.

I can fully accept myself and get a lot out of life, even with a flawed house. Here's a golden opportunity to practice working on accepting myself unconditionally, in spite of my flawed behavior and in spite of criticism from others. It's unfortunate that my house is deficient, but it's not awful, terrible, or horrible.

F. (new **F**eeling): Concern and mild disappointment rather than hurt or depression.

## *From Self-Rating to Self-Acceptance*

The goal of feeling good about your *self* is a trap: if people criticize you or if you don't live up to your standards, you see yourself as worthless and start to feel hopeless. And when you perform well in the eyes of yourself or others, you tend to think you must continue to prove yourself to maintain your self-esteem; so you feel insecure even when you're doing well.

You can use the techniques described in this chapter to root out your basic problem—self-rating. Instead of rating yourself, accept yourself just as you are—a fallible human who can enjoy life no matter how poorly you perform, and no matter who disapproves.

# 4

## *Marriage: Vicious and Delicious Circles*

*Marriages are said to be made in Heaven, which may be why they don't work here on Earth.*
— THOMAS SZASZ, *The Untamed Tongue*

Like most married couples, Carol and Steve agreed perfectly on what was wrong with their marriage—the other person's reprehensible behavior.

As they entered my office for the first time, I immediately noticed their physical resemblance—they could have passed for brother and sister. They were both lean, dark-haired, and smartly dressed.

I introduced myself and offered a friendly handshake. They both responded mechanically and without warmth. Both answered my questions sullenly and refused to be drawn into free-flowing conversation.

In their answers, they accused each other of various relationship crimes. Carol, 32, was trying to balance a new career with raising a young child. She complained bitterly that Steve rarely talked to her, was over-involved in his work, and spent too many evenings away from home. She sounded distant, as though she had already given up the relationship.

Steve, a year older than Carol, was a family practice physician. He lamented that Carol no longer responded to his amorous advances, never took his child-rearing advice seriously, and was under the thumb of her mother. He sounded hurt and betrayed.

## Something Only You Can Do

I plunged in and gave them their first lesson in healthy relating and emoting, just as it was explained by the Roman philosopher Epictetus over 2,000 years ago: Only *you* can upset yourself about events. *The events themselves, no matter how obnoxious, can never upset you.*

"But when my wife rejects my sexual advances night after night, month after month, that's very, very disappointing," Steve interrupted, sitting on his anger.

"Yes, it is," I said supportively.

"In fact it's infuriating," Steve added, getting more visibly upset.

"You *choose* to infuriate yourself about it," I corrected, holding my ground. Now he began to get angry with *me*.

"I *choose* to infuriate myself about it? Carol's the one who *chooses* which TV channel to watch all night," Steve replied sarcastically.

"Yes, but you choose your reaction to that. Suppose a hundred husbands like you all had wives like Carol, who rejected their sexual advances every night. Would all one hundred of them be equally upset?"

"Well maybe not equally. Even I'm in a forgiving mood at times," Steve said thoughtfully, his anger diminishing.

"Right. Some would be even angrier than you. Others would feel about equally as angry. Some would feel only mildly angry. And one or two would just feel keenly disappointed, without becoming angry at all."

"I think I see what you mean."

"And *you can choose* to feel keenly disappointed without becoming furious."

Like most people, Steve wasn't immediately convinced of this, but he was intrigued enough to give the idea a chance.

## Taking the "Must" Out of Your Marriage

Suppose that you, like Carol and Steve, and most human beings on the surface of this planet, believe that your partner is upsetting you. What can you do? You can tackle the problem in three stages:

1. Take responsibility for your upset;

2. Identify your "musts";

3. Dispute your "musts."

1. *Take responsibility for your upset.* Face the fact that no one else can ever upset you. Only you can upset yourself. No one can get into your gut and churn it up. Only you can do that, by the way you think.

2. *Identify your "musts."* Once you have fully acknowledged that only you can upset your own emotions, identify precisely what you're telling yourself. The culprit can usually be found in one of the three basic "musts":

   • "Must" #1 (a demand on oneself): "I MUST do well by my mate and get her approval, or I'm no good."

   • "Must" #2 (a demand on others): "My mate MUST treat me well, or she's no good."

- "Must" #3 (a demand on situations, or on The Universe): "The relationship MUST go well, or life's no good."

Try to discover what you're demanding of yourself, your partner, and your relationship. Not until you've identified your key "must" can you most effectively reduce your distress. As is often the case with feuding couples, Steve's and Carol's self-defeating thinking included all three "musts."

Steve's "must" #1: "Because Carol is rejecting me, that conclusively proves what I've always suspected—that I'm just not good enough for her and will never have the loving, supportive wife that I MUST have."

Carol's "must" #1: "I MUST have Steve's undivided attention, and if I don't get it that means he doesn't care for me at all and that I'm worthless."

Steve's "must" #2: "Since I'm her husband and she's my wife, and I feel like having sex, she MUST always comply or else she's a louse and deserves to roast in hell."

Carol's "must" #2: "Steve SHOULD spend more time at home with the family, and he's a louse because he doesn't."

Steve's "must" #3: "The relationship MUST provide me with sexual satisfaction whenever I desire it, and I CAN'T STAND being frustrated when I'm horny."

> Carol's "must" #3: "The marriage MUST last forever and never have significant problems, or else life is awful, terrible, and horrible."

3. *Dispute your "musts."* Question and challenge those beliefs which are upsetting you. Once you've exposed your "musts" to the pitiless light of day, ruthlessly attack them.

The only reason you could remain disturbed about marital problems is that you are vigorously and persistently telling yourself nonsense about them. Change that warped view to a "must"-free one, and the emotional disturbance will probably diminish, or even vanish.

You make that change by asking yourself, in writing or in your head, again and again: "What is the evidence for that "must," "awful," or "can't stand it?"

Steve did ask himself—in the form of written Three Minute Exercises—"What is the evidence I MUST have an invariably supportive wife?" "What is the evidence she MUST comply with all my sexual requests?" "What is the evidence the relationship MUST provide me with total satisfaction?"

And he concluded, over and over: "No damned evidence. No reason I HAVE TO have an ever-supportive wife, since she may choose not to support me at times. She doesn't always HAVE TO comply with my sexual requests, since I don't run the universe. The relationship doesn't HAVE TO provide me with total satisfaction since life and relationships often consist of one hassle after another."

Here, in one of Steve's Three Minute Exercises, is how he reached some of those conclusions:

## *Steve's Three Minute Exercise*

A. (**A**ctivating event): Carol rejects my sexual advances.

B. (irrational **B**elief): She MUST have sex with me whenever I want it.

C. (emotional **C**onsequence): Anger, fury, rage.

D. (**D**isputing): Why MUST she have sex with me whenever I want it?

E. (**E**ffective new thinking): There's no law of the universe stating Carol MUST have sex with me whenever I want it. I strongly prefer she does, but I don't run the universe and I can't control her inclinations.

Since she's an independent human being with free will and free choice, she may decide not to have sex at times, perhaps even much of the time. That's very unpleasant, but hardly a horror. Although I distinctly do not like cold, unsexy behavior in my wife, I can stand what I don't like.

Rather than eating myself up inside about it, I had better face the fact once and for all that whenever I make an advance, Carol may reject me. How unfortunate! But in reality, the cost of enjoying the advantages of any marriage consists of suffering the disadvantages. I can accept that.

F. (new **F**eeling): Displeasure rather than anger.

## *How Vicious Circles Work*

Nearly all serious marital problems involve vicious circles. A vicious circle arises when one partner's response to the other partner's unwelcome behavior actually encourages more of that unwelcome behavior. In the case of Carol and Steve, one vicious circle went like this:

1.  Steve didn't like the infrequency of sex with Carol.

2.  Steve chose to react by trying to pressure Carol into having sex, by displaying coldness and hostility when this didn't work, by spending less time with Carol, and by being less inclined to share concerns with her.

3.  Carol chose to respond by being less inclined to have sex.

A vicious circle can always be described from at least two points of view. In this case, we could equally well describe it as:

1.  Carol didn't like Steve's pressuring, coldness, and staying away.

2.  Carol chose to react by less frequently agreeing to sex.

3.  Steve chose to react to less frequent sex by pressuring, coldness, and staying away.

As a result of Steve's Three Minute Exercise, some *vicious circles* were replaced by *delicious circles*. As Steve succeeded in reducing his resentment about Carol's lack of sexual interest, Carol interpreted Steve as less antagonistic and more supportive. Much to Steve's delight, sex became more frequent.

Steve then became more interested in spending more time with Carol and stopped devoting such long hours to work. Steve became more comfortable with sharing things with her. They talked things over more often, and Carol began to feel more comfortable about not always conforming to her mother's wishes. She began to let Steve have his way more often with the kids' upbringing. These events began a process in which Carol and Steve abandoned their resentment of each other, became more affectionate, and gave up any thought of ending their relationship.

## *It Takes Two to Tangle*

In any vicious circle, each partner plays a necessary role. It follows that a vicious circle can be broken by either partner's unilateral act. In this case, the vicious circle could have been broken by Steve unilaterally behaving in more desirable ways toward Carol, or it could have been broken by Carol deciding to agree to sex more often. This doesn't mean that the outcome would be equally satisfactory for both parties, but either party *can* halt the vicious circle.

## *Some Common Vicious Circles*

1. Sheila wants Mark to talk to her more and tells him so.
2. Mark feels criticized.
3. Mark clams up.

<br>

1. Charmaine thinks that Victor has become less interested in sex.

2. Charmaine gets used to this idea, draws back, and becomes less physically affectionate.
3. Victor notices this behavior of Charmaine's, and also draws back.

1. Frank often works late at the office.
2. Alice feels slighted and acts more coolly to Frank.
3. Frank feels that home is a less welcoming place, and becomes more inclined to work late at the office.

1. Andrea criticizes her lover Holly for not giving positive feedback.
2. Holly feels resentful at being criticized.
3. Holly becomes even less inclined to give Andrea positive feedback.

1. Bill feels hurt by Jennifer's insistent scolding.
2. Bill reacts by becoming quiet and withdrawn.
3. Exasperated by Bill's unresponsive behavior, Jennifer tries to "get through to him" by scolding him more sharply and more frequently.

1. Ruth is tormented by the thought that Harold has his mind on other women.
2. Ruth chooses to react by always being ready to pounce on Harold, sharply monitoring the direction of his eyes and his thoughts.
3. Harold doesn't like receiving this suspicious attention, and finds consolation in day-dreaming about other women.

## *Applying Problem Separation to Vicious Circles*

A reader of my "Ask Dr. Mike" column recently presented me with this common marital dilemma: "My husband puts in such long hours at work that I rarely see him. When I do, he has nothing to say. I'm feeling resentful and hurt. Can you help me?"

I told this reader that she had two very different problems. Her Practical Problem was how to get her husband to spend more time with her and be more communicative. Her Emotional Problem was that she was unnecessarily upsetting herself.

I advised her to begin by tackling her Emotional Problem. It always has at its core some demand—of herself, another person, or a situation.

Her thinking went something like this: "My husband SHOULD spend more time with me. He MUST care for me. I SHOULD not allow him to treat me this way. I MUST do something to rekindle his love for me." It was this kind of unreasonableness—fueled by her "musts" and "shoulds"—that was upsetting her, not her husband's displeasing actions.

She would cease to be distraught if she changed her beliefs, getting rid of her "shoulds" and "musts." She would view her plight differently if she said: "I strongly PREFER my husband spend more time with me, but I'm determined to enjoy my own projects when he's not around. I don't LIKE it when he ignores me, but I don't run the universe and I don't control him. I keenly DESIRE that he treat me better, but I'm never a worm, even if he doesn't. I certainly WOULD LIKE to influence him, so I will act determinedly, not desperately."

This more realistic thinking would be the best bet for solving her Emotional Problem. I advised her next to attack her practical problem systematically:

1. Make a concerted effort to discuss the issue with your husband. Convey your concern and find out how he feels about it.

2. In later discussions, suggest various remedies to the problem until you find some he is willing to try. For instance, have him tell you about his day or ask you about yours, discuss plans for future shared evenings, weekends, or vacations, or reminisce about past times together.

3. Even if he is at first unwilling to consider any modifications or talk at all, persist in bringing it up.

If after some concerted effort you still get nowhere, consider other approaches:

1. Court him, and make the relationship so heavenly he decides to improve.

2. Suggest a deal, whereby you agree to alter some of your behaviors, in exchange for him agreeing to alter some of his.

3. Assume he'll never reform, and just improve your own life.

4. Coolly assess the prudence of divorce. If the minuses of the marriage outweigh the pluses, and if this cannot be changed, divorce is the logical option. In that case, give an ultimatum as a last resort (and be prepared to stick to it), something like: 'Although I love you, unless you take this seriously, or make changes, or get therapy, I'm leaving.' "

"If, while attempting the above strategies, you find yourself becoming resentful, angry, or hurt, that means you are again creating emotional issues out of practical ones. Use the same technique again: Find your unrealistic 'should' or 'must,' then confront and refute it, kick it out, and resolutely return to implementing your problem-solving strategies."

Often, people who take this advice find that their Practical Problem quickly becomes a whole lot easier. Once they start to question the *demand* that underlies their Emotional Problem, they may cease playing out one of the steps in a vicious circle. The woman reader, for example, may well have reacted to her husband's staying away with some behavior that encouraged him to stay away. This behavior might include yelling at him, becoming tearful, or withholding sex. Once she recognizes her belief that he MUST spend more time with her to be pure foolishness, she may find herself easing back on some of these unhelpful responses.

However, the method of separating Emotional and Practical Problems is the best method, regardless of whether it also breaks a vicious circle. The possibility does exist that the other person's behavior will not improve, even if you start to behave more rationally! But acting rationally is still the best policy.

## A Disagreeable Duo

Donald and Donna agreed that their marriage was rapidly going down the tubes. When they spoke to each other in my office, they were both tight-lipped and reserved, Donald slightly defiant in his manner, and Donna quivering with injured dignity.

They had met while working at a small software company and had been married for three and a half stormy years before they finally came to me for counseling. Donald sported a trim blond beard and a lean and hungry look, while Donna carried 20 extra pounds.

Donald described himself as enjoying hard work. He frequently stayed late at the office. In addition, he was currently immersed in two other projects: adding a porch to their house and restoring his boat.

He complained that Donna felt like a failure and kept letting him know it. She was usually depressed, yet always had to have the last word. Donna, he said, would pressure him and get angry whenever he didn't immediately take her hints to do needed chores around the house.

"She cuts me up and tells me I'm a failure. She tries to control me by telling me exactly how to run my life. She rants and raves when I don't do every little thing her way, and then I get depressed and feel as though I have to walk on eggshells to avoid an emotional explosion."

I turned to Donna, who seemed to be seething with suppressed emotion: "And what's your side?"

She responded tersely that he had become more contentious lately. In the middle of an argument he would raise his voice, swear, kick, and punch things. He was unreliable, promising to fix things and then never getting to them. When he did work on some project, he would always leave a terrible mess. He was cold and indifferent except for sex, and he would always favor his own kids over hers.

Donna abruptly stopped talking and stared sullenly into space, fighting back tears. Since an emotional catharsis in the office would prove a waste of their valuable time and money, I offered Donna a tissue but continued my dialogue with Donald.

## *Counseling Half a Couple*

Donna didn't return after the first session, so I worked on the marriage with Donald alone. It was a bit like swimming with one hand tied behind my back—slow, difficult, and quite a challenge, with a diminished chance of total success. However, I explained to Donald about vicious circles and how one person could often improve matters by breaking the circle.

Later, I encouraged Donald to keep a "therapy notebook," divided into various sections with titles such as "Irrational Beliefs," "Situations where I get upset," and "Undesirable emotions I experience."

Over the next few weeks, Donald collected a number of his "Irrational Beliefs":

- Donna SHOULD not continually pressure me!

- She MUST not cut me up!

- Life OUGHT not to consist of unnecessary problems!

- Donna SHOULD never say I'm a failure!

- I SHOULD not have to restrict myself!

- I MUST not upset Donna, and it's AWFUL when she becomes so hostile and weepy!

- Donna SHOULD not try to control my life!

- I HAVE TO help the kids, or I'm a louse!

- I MUST make the relationship succeed!

- Donna MUST not punish me for not doing things her way!

- My ex-wife MUST not endanger my relationship with the kids!

Over the next few sessions, Donald and I devised these homework assignments to improve the marriage:

1. Write out a Three Minute Exercise every day and bring the past seven days' output to me every week.

2. Give Donna positive feedback every day.

3. Speak to Donna without swearing.

4. Speak to Donna without raising my voice.

5. Speak to Donna without kicking or punching things.

6. Go along with her nutty demands whenever possible, and when not possible, don't become excited about it.

7. Calmly do my own thing at times.

8. Set up conversation times with Donna.

9. Push myself to show affection to Donna, especially when I don't feel like it.

10. Read *How to Live with a Neurotic* by Albert Ellis.

11. Remind myself twice a day of the bottom line: "I'm doing it for me."

12. Implement the above strategies for four months, then leave if they don't work.

## *Donald's Three Minute Exercise*

A. (**A**ctivating event): Donna seems angry at me for something I did, but I haven't the foggiest notion of what.

B. (irrational **B**elief): I MUST not upset Donna. It's AWFUL she's so upset. I'm a skunk.

C. (emotional **C**onsequences): Depression. Walking on eggshells.

D. (**D**isputing): Why MUST I not upset Donna? How is it AWFUL she's so upset? How am I a skunk?

E. (**E**ffective new thinking): Although I prefer not to distress Donna, no law of the universe states that I MUST not distress Donna. At worst I'm an imperfect person acting imperfectly, not a skunk.

Being human and fallible, Donna will disturb herself when she chooses to. I'm not in control of that. It's sad that she does that to herself, but not the end of the world. She has angered herself in the past and survived, and unfortunately will anger herself in the future, but will probably survive. Depressing myself about it just makes matters worse, and doesn't help Donna.

By philosophically accepting that all relationships have their difficulties, that another relationship might have fewer (or more) hassles, but never zero, I will diminish the distress I've been creating for myself.

As long as the advantages of this relationship outweigh the disadvantages, it would be wise to hang in while attempting to improve it, and minimize my unrealistic notions about it.

F.  (new **F**eeling): Regret rather than depression. Being myself rather than walking on eggshells.
During the four-month trial period, Donald succeeded at softening his stubbornness, acting more attentively, giving Donna positive feedback, and greatly reducing his tantrums.

For her part, Donna appeared to become overtly less critical, but did not change significantly enough to make the relationship worth it for Donald.

It's difficult for most individuals to be untroubled simply living with *themselves.* When two people attempt a partnership together, their problems are often compounded. However, when couples conscientiously use the Three Minute Therapy approach, they dramatically increase their chances of having a fulfilling relationship.

# 5

# *Anger: The High Price of Losing Your Cool*

> *His Holiness The Dalai Lama was asked whether it was ever useful or legitimate to get angry with someone else. He sat in silence for several minutes, exactly like a chess player meditating on the consequences of all the possible moves, and then, having exhausted all the possibilities, he simply said, "No."*
> —GUY CLAXTON, *The Heart of Buddhism*

Alvin, a 53-year-old lawyer, came to me because of his miserable marriage. He said that he often had heated rows with his wife, Peggy, who frequently nagged him and complained. He also reported bitterly that Peggy would never keep the house clean enough or prepare meals as he would like them prepared. Upon discussion, it turned out that he judged his wife's performance by perfectionist standards. Although Alvin said he was finding his marriage intolerable, he revealed, in answer to my questions, that he most definitely did not want a divorce and was afraid that Peggy would leave him.

## *A Demanding Spouse*

What was really wrong with Alvin's marriage? Since she frequently complained and threatened to leave, I asked Alvin what Peggy was so unhappy about.

"I don't know," he replied sullenly.

"Well," I asked him, "if she were here right now, what would *she* say was making her so unhappy?"

"That I'm always correcting her."

"And do you always correct her?"

In answer to this, Alvin irritably began again to recite his wife's shortcomings, especially her failure to clean and cook to his satisfaction. The root of Alvin's problem was his anger at his wife, which sprang from his demandingness.

Alvin was not at first aware that he was a demander. However, there was a pattern visible in his remarks about his wife. This pattern implied that he was ruler of the universe and his wife his subject. Such an outlook is, of course, ludicrous, but it was implicit in Alvin's tone of injured resentment and the uncompromising way he described the issues between them.

Made explicit, Alvin's attitude amounted to the following:

- Peggy MUST keep the house clean, and she deserves to be punished because she doesn't

- Peggy OUGHT to prepare meals just the way I want them

- Peggy SHOULD understand me (By "understanding" him, Alvin meant that she should agree with his point of view.)

Underlying these demands, preferences that reflected Alvin's tastes, values, and hopes were evident:

- I WOULD LIKE the house cleaned and the food prepared to my specifications, and it's disappointing that it's not

- I PREFER that Peggy see things my way

Alvin has a legitimate right to such preferences. His preferences weren't his emotional problem. Alvin's disturbance arose when he escalated his subjective preferences into godlike commands: "Because I'd love it if you kept the house cleaner, prepared meals to my taste and didn't hassle me, you MUST do as I say!"

Alvin had an attitude very common in troubled marriages: "Why should I be the one to change? If she treated me better, I wouldn't be so upset. She SHOULD be the one to change." I persuaded Alvin—and he took a lot of persuading—that this attitude was irrelevant and impractical. If he did not want a divorce, then he was stuck with Peggy, and realistically there was no likelihood that she would start behaving according to his ideal picture of how she "should" behave.

Alvin's "musts" were without foundation. No reason exists that Peggy or anyone else MUST do as Alvin likes. If Alvin actually did run the universe, with Peggy as his slave, his demandingness would have been reasonable. You might think it was pretty crazy for Alvin to view himself—a very limited, imperfect person—as ruler of the universe. *Yet such a view is the essence of all anger.*

## A Disabling Emotion

Anger is not an involuntary emotional response to a specific situation. Anger arises from a philosophy—a way of viewing the world. At its core, anger represents an outlook of grandiosity, self-righteousness, commanding, and condemning.

Many mental health professionals disagree with this view, that all kinds of anger are generally bad for you.

## Anger: The High Price of Losing Your Cool

Most therapists classify anger as "appropriate" or "inappropriate" according to context, and they usually argue that, when appropriate, it is healthy to express anger ("let it out") and unhealthy to suppress anger ("bottle it up").

Recent research, however, contradicts this popular view, and suggests that all anger, expressed or suppressed, is harmful to your health and damaging to your relationships with other people. Among the many difficulties associated with anger are:

- Increased likelihood of heart attack, stroke, and hypertension

- Greater difficulty in solving problems constructively

- A tendency for the anger, which may start in one area of your life, to overlap and extend into other areas

- Preoccupation with thoughts of revenge

- Adopting an antagonistic attitude which needlessly alienates other people with whom it's advantageous to have cordial dealings

- A predisposition to violence, especially child abuse

*But doesn't expressing anger help release a lot of pent-up frustration?* It's true that an outburst of anger may sometimes momentarily provide relief. But psychological distress often takes its toll on the body, and some preliminary evidence suggests that expressed anger causes more physical damage than suppressed anger. There is, however, a third alternative to suppressing or expressing your anger: Don't make yourself angry in the first place!

The "expressive" approach implies that anger is something inside you, like a gallbladder. If your gallbladder bothers you, you could have it removed, and then it won't bother you anymore. Similarly, if you can get your anger out, it won't be inside you any more, causing distress.

This view is hopelessly mistaken. Anger is not a physical entity. It's a feeling generated by an attitude or belief. You don't free yourself of feelings by expressing the attitudes and beliefs that create them. That usually reaffirms and strengthens those attitudes and thus makes the feeling more likely to return.

Consider an opposite sort of feeling, like love—a feeling that we often want to continue. It's clear that the more you express feelings of love, tenderness, and caring, the more loving, tender, and caring you are likely to become. No one would suppose that by expressing such feelings you were "letting them out" and thus losing them.

It's exactly the same with the self-destructive feeling of anger. If you express your anger, you reaffirm and solidify your angry attitude, and make it more difficult to dispel. If you refrain from expressing your anger, this may be the first step towards avoiding anger entirely.

## Problems With a Preteen

In my psychotherapy practice I continually encounter people with hostility problems: parents angry at their kids, kids angry at their parents, and husbands and wives angry at each other—and at their lovers, not to mention their spouses' lovers.

Leanne was 41 and had a 12-year-old daughter, Sally. Leanne came to see me because she was afraid she might one day explode at Sally's delinquent behavior. Sally was playing hooky and lying with increasing frequency.

"I can't understand why Sally lies like she does. After promising every night that she'll go to school next morning, she doesn't do a thing about it."

I asked Leanne what she was doing to help Sally get going in the morning.

"Well, I tell her that if she doesn't get to school I'm going to murder her."

"I see. And how does she respond to that?"

"She pulls the covers over her head and pretends to be asleep."

"How do you feel at that moment?"

"I start to boil inside."

"Where does it get you to boil inside?"

"Where does it get me? Here, I guess."

"That's right. Your anger hasn't accomplished a thing with Sally. Even worse, you're working yourself into a frazzle."

"Yeah, I am. I am."

"And it seems that the more you rant and rave in the morning, the more Sally tries to escape under her covers."

"You're right, I guess. But I just don't know what else to do. I'm beside myself."

The first objective with people in Leanne's situation is to help them clearly understand that they are making *themselves* angry, and that their anger causes additional problems for them.

Leanne had a *practical* problem: what to do about her daughter. Her *emotional* problem was her anger. I managed to convince Leanne that once she had tackled her anger, she would then be better placed to do something about her *practical* problem.

Eventually, after Leanne had trained herself to avoid anger, we worked out a feasible strategy for changing her daughter's behavior through a system of rewards and penalties. For example, if Sally got up on time one morning, she would be allowed to watch a desired video that evening.

It turned out that the idea had already occurred to Leanne of using rewards and penalties, and she had even attempted this, but she had not been consistent because of her anger. Effective bribery requires a cool head.

## *Delays, Demands, and Distress*

Heather, a 35-year-old woman with long blonde hair and a woebegone look, consulted me because she frequently felt melancholy and lacking in motivation.

"I never feel like getting out of bed in the morning," she told me sorrowfully. "I just don't feel that anything's worthwhile." As well as feeling generally depressed, Heather often became seriously upset and prone to fits of weeping.

After careful questioning, I concluded that Heather's dissatisfaction was mostly focused on her six-year-old marriage. In most respects, the marriage seemed fine. Heather's husband Peter was loving, supportive, and communicative. But she felt she just could not stand his compulsive lateness.

As long as she had known Peter, he had never gotten to appointments on time. As much as he apologized and resolved to be prompt thereafter, he always appeared at best twenty minutes late. Needless to say, this created serious problems, not only for himself but also for Heather. In addition to being late for movies and social engagements, Heather missed flights and first acts of plays because of him.

Over the years Heather had tried a number of strategies. For a while she refused to go anywhere with him, but that practically destroyed their social life. Helping him get ready was a failure because he claimed she was underfoot and delaying him even further. Constantly prodding and reminding him only seemed to make him more prone to lateness, and always ended with Heather having a temper tantrum. She tried lying about the times of appointments, and once or twice this worked, but it ended by giving Peter an additional reason to be late: he began to factor her lying into his calculations and to estimate that the true time of an appointment was later than she said it was.

In response to my questions, Heather admitted with great embarrassment that because of Peter's chronic lateness, she was resenting him to the point where she was seriously considering divorce.

Heather's *practical* problem was that she was often inconvenienced by her husband's lateness. Her *emotional* problem was that she was making herself miserable because of the anger she directed against her husband.

Heather's demands included:

- Peter MUST treat me more considerately

- He MUST be on time

- He MUST not ruin my plans

- He MUST not keep my friends waiting

- He SHOULD be more caring

- Because he is so responsible in other areas of his life, he SHOULD act more responsibly in this area

During my second session with Heather, I taught her the Three Minute Exercise method. She proved to be one of my more conscientious clients, and for a while was practicing the Three Minute Exercises three times a day. As her thinking became more realistic, her anger diminished.

Eventually she was able to do fewer Three Minute Exercises yet still not upset herself about the inconvenience Peter was imposing on her. She then weighed the pros and cons of her marriage more realistically and decided that Peter's advantages considerably outweighed his disadvantages.

## *Heather's Three Minute Exercise*

Here's an example of one of the many Three Minute Exercises that Heather wrote out and thought through until she had thoroughly uprooted her "musts."

A. (**A**ctivating event): Peter treats me inconsiderately by arriving 30 minutes late for our appointment.

B. (irrational **B**elief): Peter MUST treat me more considerately.

C. (emotional **C**onsequences): Anger, fury, rage.

D. (**D**isputing): Why MUST he treat me more considerately?

E. (**E**ffective new thinking): There's no law of the universe stating that Peter MUST treat me more considerately. I strongly prefer that he does, but I don't run the universe and I can't control Peter. Since he's an imperfect human with free will and free choice, he's going to act inconsiderately at times. Everyone is imperfect, and persistent lateness is Peter's kind of imperfection. That's very unpleasant but hardly a horror! Although I distinctly do not like such inconsiderate behavior, I can stand what I don't like. Rather than eating myself up inside about it, I had better face the fact once and for all that whenever we make an appointment with anyone, the probability is that Peter will be late. How unfortunate! But the reality is that enjoying the advantages of my marriage means also suffering the disadvantages.

F. (new **F**eeling): Displeasure rather than anger.

Two months of therapy helped Heather feel more accepting of Peter's problem. However, she did occasionally experience brief setbacks by demanding that Peter be better at keeping appointments. But immediately, without fail, she took out paper and pencil and did a Three Minute Exercise. These few minutes of concentrated reflection changed her anger to simply keen displeasure about living with the problem.

## How to Be Cool

Dealing with your own anger, resentment, or hostility involves three steps:

1. First, admit that *you* are making yourself angry. No other person, experience, or situation is. You can recognize that a person, experience, or situation is unpleasant or undesired. That alone doesn't explain or justify your anger. No matter how obnoxious the object of your dislike may be, the anger is your responsibility. It is *never* warranted by external circumstances.

2  Second, identify the demand you are making—the "must" or the "should" you are inventing in-

side your head—which is leading to your anger about the frustrating person or situation.

3. Finally, question and dispute this demand *ad nauseum*, until it loses all plausibility.

## Dealing with Difficult People

I can already hear some readers objecting: "Is Heather supposed to put up with this inconsiderate behavior? Are you telling us we have to be meek and mild?"

People who try to justify anger usually speak as though the only alternative to anger is to be passively "meek and mild." But in fact, other alternatives are available, such as calm assertiveness or reasoned compliance. Here are some examples:

- A state trooper awarding a speeding ticket is typically neither angry nor passive. He is calm, firm, and assertive.

- A professional boxer is not "meek and mild" in the ring, but he is generally not angry. (He may sometimes calculatedly taunt his opponent, if he thinks that the opponent may get angry and thereby become less effective.)

- An army private is rather compliant in the face of her sergeant's commands. It would simply be foolish for her to behave otherwise, for example, to angrily protest: "I'm a sensitive, feeling individual, so consider my uniqueness before ordering me around." A policy of calculated compliance is usually best with most bosses, when dealing directly with the IRS, or with any other very powerful organization that has the ability to harm you.

## *Meekness is One Useful Strategy*

But still, readers may want to challenge my advice to Heather: "Surely people like Peter can be made to change their bad habits! Surely Heather has every right to be angry! Are you proposing the other-worldly notion of 'turning the other cheek'? Are we supposed to let people walk all over us and never fight back?"

At first all this sounds like a reasonable response, but it frequently serves as a flimsy justification for anger and irrational demanding. Suppose you are confronted by a "difficult" person. Let's carefully consider some aspects of the problem:

1. It *may* just be that there really is "nothing you can do" (nothing that won't have far more undesirable consequences than putting up with the other person's obnoxious behavior). If there really is nothing you can do, then you had better calmly face that fact.

2. It may be that your only real choice is to leave or stay. If you decide it's best to leave the other person, then why not leave unangrily? (When people look back later on the furious rows that occurred at the time a relationship was terminated, they are often glad the relationship was terminated, but they nearly always regret the angry scenes.) If you decide to stay, then you accept the probability that he will continue his obnoxious behavior. Either way, anger doesn't help. Either way, anger is causing you additional

problems. And either way, you are more likely to make the best decision about staying or leaving if you *first* get rid of your anger and accept the other person's behavior for the time being.

3. If there *is* something you can do (other than leaving), it will not be helped by being angry, and being angry will probably reduce your effectiveness at doing it. (If it's really true—and this is quite exceptional—that *showing* anger will be effective in getting the other person to do what you want and will not have worse consequences for you, then it's better to keep a cool head and *pretend* to be angry.)

4. If you get rid of your anger and calm down, you can more realistically survey the available options. You can rationally experiment with different tactics for changing the other person. Remember, getting rid of your anger does *not* mean liking what used to make you angry, nor does it mean being resigned to it.

5. If the other person's undesirable behavior is of long standing, then there's a strong possibility that he will never change, and if he ever does change it may be slowly, or it may not happen for some years. Even if you hope that he may change significantly in the near future, it would be unwise to assume that he will.

6. Very often the kind of behavior that flows from anger is almost the worst possible way to get the result you would like. For example, ranting and raving at someone is very rarely an efficacious method for improving their behavior. It usually leads to resistance and resentment in the other

person. Even if you are also doing something effective to get him to change, your displays of anger will probably retard his progress.

7. Surprisingly often, angry behavior fuels the other person's unpleasant behavior (See the discussion of vicious circles in chapter 4). You may find that, simply because you are calm and reasoned all the time, the other person will spontaneously start to improve. Of course, this may not happen, but it happens often enough to be worth mentioning.

8. Sometimes a consistent display of love and affection (or, in the case of a non-intimate relationship, of amiable respect) is effective in modifying the other person's obnoxious behavior. Angry feelings would almost certainly sabotage that effort.

9. Yes, Heather does have a *right* to be angry. We all have a perfect right to be foolish in any number of ways.

10. There are some circumstances where turning the other cheek may be an effective method for resolving a problem. It's a bad idea to make 'turning the other cheek' into an absolute principle. But where it might work, why not try it?

You may be wondering what happened to Heather. Accepting the reality of Peter's lateness and avoiding anger, she became much less distressed. After several months in which she demonstrated that she did not demand that Peter MUST be on time for appointments, she was able to discuss with him, in a calm and good-humored way, different possibilities for coping with his lateness. One method—

more symbolic than anything else—was for him to pay her a fine of one dollar for every minute he was late. After some weeks of this, Peter's lateness was still a problem, but the average time late had been reduced, and occasionally he would appear on time, much to the pleasure of both of them. Finally, Peter became a client of mine and successfully tackled his lateness. (For his first three therapy sessions he turned up very late—I callously billed him for the time.)

## The Case of the Repulsive Relative

Ernie, 28, had a good marriage with a first baby on the way. He came to me because of his anger problem—he described himself as having "a short fuse." Ernie was a well-liked "captain" (head waiter) at an elegant New York restaurant, yet he was almost fired on two occasions when he exploded at customers who, he complained, were playing "head games" with him.

Over the course of his five years in that job, Ernie generally got along well with his manager. On unexpectedly busy nights, she would sometimes make a last-minute request that he stay later than originally scheduled. Regrettably, Ernie responded angrily.

Worse yet, he once came upon a police officer writing him a parking ticket. In a rage, Ernie foolishly punched the policeman. What probably saved Ernie from criminal prosecution was his thin, diminutive, non-threatening appearance.

During therapy, Ernie practiced his Three Minute Exercises conscientiously, and did quite well in uprooting his anger. His wife reported to me, during a brief phone call after his fifth session, that she was gratified he was doing so well, and thanked me profusely for my help. Ernie terminated therapy after one more session.

A few months later, Ernie called for further therapy. The anger he had so successfully dealt with was rapidly reappearing. When clients have a relapse like this, my hunch is that they've stopped doing their Three Minute Exercises regularly. As a result, their "musts" creep back into their thinking. This was, in fact, what had occurred in Ernie's case.

This time, Ernie's most pressing problem involved a new protagonist. In two weeks' time Ernie's in-laws, Leroy and Gloria, would be arriving from the West Coast for their annual month-long stay. It was understandable, after I had heard his description of Leroy, that Ernie wasn't thrilled with the prospect:

"You wouldn't believe it. He's oblivious to the rest of the world. He does what he wants, when he wants to, without the slightest concern for anyone else's privacy or feelings. He's inconsiderate, thick-skulled, and he has body odor.

"Last year Gloria was seriously considering divorce, but she has her own problems. She's insecure and is afraid to leave after thirty years of marriage.

"Leroy doesn't believe in using deodorant. He claims it's unhealthy since it's made with aluminum. But he's sitting at the dinner table and he stinks. And did you ever see anyone who brushes his teeth in the living room while everyone else is watching TV? This drives me up the wall. Or he'll be talking to you and flossing his teeth. Would you believe that I can tell him that he's an idiot and curse him up and down, and it won't bother him? But he's driving me crazy.

"We were out the other day and we needed some film, so we decided to stop at one of those large chain pharmacies. Leroy was chomping down a bag of cookies and a very courteous salesclerk came over to help us. Chewing a mouthful and a half, Leroy asked for film. The salesclerk immediately recoiled, got very short with Leroy, and dispensed with him as quickly as she could.

"After we left the store I confronted Leroy: 'Do you think the salesclerk was a little brusque with you?' He admitted that he had noticed it. But when I asked him why he thought she was, he hadn't the foggiest notion. I gave him my interpretation and he sort of acknowledged that I might be right, but showed no interest in changing. I blew my stack."

We then uncovered some of Ernie's "musts":

- Leroy MUST show some interest in making his behavior less unpleasant to others

- Leroy MUST act like a respectable human being

- Leroy MUST not be so dense

- Leroy MUST not be an embarrassment in public

- Leroy MUST not be a slob

## Ernie's Three Minute Exercise

Here is one of the many Three Minute Exercises that Ernie did:

A. (**A**ctivating event): Leroy shows no interest in changing his obnoxious behavior.

B. (irrational **B**elief): Leroy MUST see things my way, the right way.

C. (emotional **C**onsequence): Anger.

D. (**D**isputing): Why MUST Leroy see things my way?

E. (**E**ffective new thinking): It would be wonderful if Leroy saw things my way, but no clause in the U.S. Constitution says that he MUST. I distinctly do not like it when he acts inconsiderately, but I can stand what I don't like. Since he's human, that means he's very imperfect, so I can expect him to act imperfectly and even idiotically. Since I don't run the universe, I don't control Leroy. He has free will and free choice so he'll act the way he chooses, not the way I think he MUST. It will be very unpleasant living with him for a month, but not awful, terrible, or horrible. Ripping myself up inside hurts me much more than his obnoxious behavior ever could. At worst, his boorishness would only be a great pain in the ass, but would not give me the high blood pressure that I'm giving to myself. And if it gets worse than I care to put up with, I could tell him to stay at a motel or deny my home to him for future visits.

F. (new **F**eeling): Very displeased and frustrated, not angry.

Ernie quickly got back into the habit of spending three minutes each day on writing his Three Minute Exercises. He thereby minimized his own agitation about Leroy's obnoxious behavior.

Ernie continued to find Leroy highly objectionable to live with, but realized he wasn't likely to influence Leroy single-handedly. So Ernie and I devised a two-part strategy to persuade Leroy to seek therapy.

Ernie began to remind Leroy repeatedly of all the people he was annoying or alienating, including his wife Gloria, his daughter (Ernie's wife), friends, business associates, and sales help. Now that Ernie was over his anger, he felt able to deliver an ultimatum to Leroy without flying into a rage: Either modify your obnoxious habits or stay elsewhere next year.

Leroy accepted Ernie's ultimatum, reluctantly sought therapy, and rather begrudgingly started to change. Soon, Leroy began to notice the somewhat pleased comments he received from those who knew him, and he became a little more enthusiastic about changing.

Leroy has not transformed his entire personality, but he has changed enough to make living with him for one month each year a relatively pleasant experience for Ernie and his wife.

# 6

## *Procrastination: The Easy Road to a Stressful Life*

*I never put off until tomorrow what I can possibly put off until the day after tomorrow.*
—OSCAR WILDE (1856–1900)

Betty was a delicate-featured, raven-haired woman in her mid-thirties. She came to see me because of recurring bouts of depression; it was easy to observe that her conversation readily turned to her own inadequacies. For example, although she was slender, elegantly proportioned, and decidedly above average in general physical appearance, she frequently and casually referred to herself as "fat" and "disgusting." It was difficult for me to avoid the impression that I was being preached to by a dedicated and fanatical missionary. Betty's gospel was that she was a washout and a miserable failure in everything she did.

Betty was married with three children. Two years before she saw me, she had given up a well-paid professional job to become a full-time homemaker, home-schooling the children, and recovering some of the lost income from employment by saving on baby-sitters' fees. As many people have discovered before and since, Betty found that looking after young children is much more, not less, demanding than a full-time office job. Not only had she made little progress with various artistic and musical endeavors she had believed she would be able to pursue, she had been unable to supplement the family income with freelance work, and she even found herself falling behind with routine tasks like paying the bills.

Betty was convinced that her failure to get things done conclusively demonstrated her trashiness as a human being. She berated herself guiltily for her procrastination. At the same time her guilt reinforced her procrastination, because she constantly reaffirmed her incompetence. Every time she failed to perform some task as promptly as she had intended, she found further "evidence" that she was doomed to procrastinate for the rest of her life.

I helped Betty fight her self-loathing, self-downing thinking with a Three Minute Exercise designed to help her realize that just because she often procrastinated unreasonably, this did not turn her into a worthless person. In this context, her habit of procrastinating was a Practical Problem, while her Emotional Problem was the self-loathing she inflicted upon herself.

Next, we turned to Betty's procrastination habit, a behavioral problem with "musty" roots. At first Betty maintained that she was simply overwhelmed with too many things to do in the limited time available. As I questioned her, it emerged that there were times in the day when she could tackle the overdue bills, when the kids were napping or comparatively quiet, but on those occasions she would find reasons not to pick up the pile of bills.

"So, when you have an opportunity to go through that pile of bills, why don't you? What reason do you give yourself for doing something else?"

"That I am too exhausted and will do a better job of paying the bills when I'm wide awake. So I choose to do something that requires no concentration, like watching TV, or I try to wake myself up by doing something physically active like sorting out the laundry."

"But you eventually do pay those old bills?"

"Yes. I usually get into a panic at two in the morning and spend the next couple of hours getting all the bills straight."

"And that makes you feel more exhausted the following day?"

"Yes," she replied miserably. "And I have to pay late fees."

Further questioning revealed that at the very moment when she put off going through the bills during the day, Betty was telling herself: "The bills MUST be paid when I'm alert, and now I'm too exhausted." Betty had a case of Low Frustration Tolerance. Because of this "must," she rebelled against doing something inherently tedious, and invented rationalizations for putting it off. Like many unreasonable procrastinators, Betty told herself: "I'll get to it when the conditions are just right." And that meant: "I'll get to it when I feel good about it."

## Betty's Three Minute Exercise

Betty addressed her unreasonable procrastination with the following Three Minute Exercise:

A. (**A**ctivating event). Two of the children are napping and the other is fairly quiet. Here's an opportunity to catch up on the bills, but I feel exhausted.

B. (irrational **B**elief): It SHOULD be easy to get myself to pay the bills.

C. (behavioral **C**onsequence): Switch on the TV.

D. (**D**isputing): Why SHOULD it be easy to get myself to pay the bills?

E. (**E**ffective new thinking): There's no reason it SHOULD be easy to get myself to pay the bills. There's no reason I SHOULD always be in a position to do just the things I feel like doing and only under perfect conditions. No good fairy is going to arrange my life so that I, alone of all people in the history of the world, am in this fortunate position. I'll feel better in an hour if I do the bills now. If I persist at these bills, I may soon feel less tired, but even when dog tired, I am intellectually capable of sorting out these bills.

Taking care of those bills now is a small investment with big returns: for the occasional twenty minutes doing something I don't like, I can avoid a future crisis when I might spend more time at a more undesirable time of day. And I will also avoid late charges.

F. (new **F**eeling and behavior): Face the bills, even though I'm exhausted, rather than watch TV.

## *Procrastination Isn't All Bad*

Unreasonable procrastination is one of the most widespread and crippling of personal problems, but very few people come to see me because they are concerned about their procrastination. When people suffer from an emotional condition, such as anxiety or depression, they may think of seeing a psychotherapist, but when people suffer from a behavioral problem, such as drinking or overeating, they rarely consider a psychotherapist. They may think of Alcoholics Anonymous, or Weight Watchers, or some other self-help group. There is, however, no Procrastinators Anonymous, although unreasonable procrastination is even more widespread than overdrinking or overeating, and often helps to cause these other problems.

Betty's case was very typical, in that she felt impelled to see a therapist because of an emotional state—depression—but it then emerged that she was bothering herself about failing to complete tasks she believed she ought to perform, and was lashing herself cruelly because of her behavioral disorder—unreasonable procrastination.

"Procrastination" comes from two Latin words meaning "for tomorrow." Procrastination simply means deferring until a later date; it is not necessarily self-defeating. To procrastinate—to delay some action—can often be a reasonable thing to do.

In isolation, an individual decision to procrastinate may be hard to classify as reasonable or unreasonable. If Richard puts off a visit to the dentist, pleading pressure of work, this may be rational. But if Richard has been using the same excuse for the past five years so that he now faces the prospect of costly gum surgery, which he could have avoided by keeping his dental appointments, we may suspect that Richard's procrastination is unreasonable.

Even the most unreasonable procrastinators can often find a plausible-sounding reason for procrastinating on each occasion. If you are in doubt about whether your decision to defer some action is reasonable or unreasonable, a good test is the No Future Regrets method: ask yourself how you will feel about your current decision when you look back on it a day or two later. When tomorrow comes, will you think today's decision was wise, or will you regret it? In most cases, it's only necessary to pose this question clearly to know the answer immediately. Then you act accordingly: you behave now in the way that you think you will look back upon with most satisfaction at a later date.

## *Colin's Procrastination Problem*

Colin was a good-looking young African-American with a friendly manner, a springy step, an impressive physique, and the musical lilt in his voice that indicated a childhood in the West Indies. He was, however, suffering from bouts of anxiety, which had grown more severe over recent months. For the first time in his life he was being troubled by insomnia, feelings of insecurity, and worries about his sexual potency.

Colin had determined some time before to make a career in business administration and had chosen the route of first studying for the CPA exam by taking a course in accounting. When he started, his natural quick-wittedness plus the novelty of the material, which held his interest, resulted in outstanding grades. However, Colin had soon come to view the course as a dull chore. The less he liked the course, the more he avoided the hours of reading and study required each week to keep up with the lectures and to follow what was going on. The more he fell behind, the more he found parts of the course difficult to follow, and so the less he liked the course.

Like much unreasonable procrastination, Colin's behavior seemed at first glance inexplicable. He declared himself fully committed to the goal of mastering the course, and he understood that this required hours of intense study each week. Yet the weeks were going by, and he was not putting in those hours. He worried about this situation and wished that he would study and once again achieve outstanding grades. Colin worked during the day as a delivery driver for a computer retail chain, and most evenings, he practiced martial arts at a local tae kwon do academy. He was a black belt and had won several trophies in competitive martial arts.

*Procrastination: The Easy Road to a Stressful Life*

Colin admitted that there were days when he thought of spending the entire evening working on his accounting studies, but he usually abandoned this idea, most often to practice martial arts. Colin accepted the popular Freudian notion that his tendency to duck out of studying must have some unconscious explanation linked with his childhood, and this wrong-headed Freudian theory made him feel helpless in the face of his procrastination.

I focused on the most recent occasion where he had put off studying:

"What did you feel at the point where you decided to forget the accounting books and go down to the gym?"

"Anxiety, fear. I dread giving up an evening to pore over books, but I really enjoy practicing martial arts and meeting my friends at the gym."

"This," I explained, "is called discomfort anxiety. You make yourself anxious about the boring work, and then you procrastinate to avoid it. You're intolerant of the discomfort of sitting down to read about straight-line depreciation. But surely you didn't start this accounting course because you thought studying would be sheer fun?"

Although Colin readily agreed that it was unreasonable to expect studying accounting to be effortless or delightful, when he actually sat down and opened the books, he began telling himself that study OUGHT NOT to be so dull, so time-consuming, and so demanding. Colin loathed his studies partly because he had fallen behind and felt guilty about this. But mainly, he feared them because he believed that studying SHOULD be fun, SHOULD be easy, and SHOULD not compete for large chunks of his time with really enjoyable activities.

I appealed to Colin's awareness of a principle he already followed in building muscles for his martial arts: No Pain, No Gain! Colin was quickly able to see that this principle applied to career goals as much as it applied to bodily strength and agility.

## Colin's Three Minute Exercise

Here is one of Colin's most effective Three Minute Exercises:

A. (**A**ctivating event): I sit down and begin to read about straight-line depreciation.

B. (irrational **B**elief): Studying accounting SHOULD not take up hours of my time and SHOULD not be so unexciting.

C. (emotional and behavioral **C**onsequences): Intense loathing for accounting theory. Leave the books and go to the gym.

D. (**D**isputing): Why SHOULD studying accounting not take up hours of my time and not be so unexciting?

E. (**E**ffective new thinking): There's simply no reason why accounting SHOULD not be time-consuming and tedious. If it were easy and fun, then everyone would have the CPA qualification and that certificate wouldn't be such a career advantage. Spending several hours a night concentrating on accounting is an investment, like building muscles or practicing martial arts techniques. No pain, no gain!

It's not the dullness of accounting that compels me to skip studying. It's what I tell myself about it. But I am capable of making myself study, and it's worth it. In fact, if I give the books fifteen minutes, I'll probably then start to feel more interested in what I'm reading, and it won't be so unappetizing for the following hour or so. And by the end of the evening I'll feel gratified at having made some progress.

F. (new **F**eeling and behavior): Reduced distaste for studying. Several hours of study accomplished each evening. Pleasure from contemplating the progress being made toward an important goal.

## *No Pain, No Gain*

Nothing of great value is ever achieved simply by doing what comes most easily. You will be effective in pursuing any important long-term goal, whether it's writing a novel or preserving your marriage, only if you work at it when you don't feel like working at it. In his martial arts, Colin was familiar with periods when he seemed to be making slow progress and when the practice seemed less enjoyable than usual. He already understood, in his purely physical pursuits, that it was most satisfying to stick to the long-term project, ignoring his day-to-day fluctuations in interest and enjoyment.

It proved helpful for Colin to extend this understanding to his progress in accounting. After a hard struggle, with some relapses, he convinced himself that he could indeed tolerate the discomfort of doing what he didn't feel like doing. When I last saw him, Colin had caught up with the rest of the class, was earning good grades again, and eagerly looked forward to gaining his CPA diploma.

## Paul's Procrastination

Paul was referred to me by his older sister. Now happily married and living in Canada, she had seen me three years ago for help with her marriage. Paul had the same large bone structure, dark wavy hair, dark eyes, dark complexion, and warm manner as she. After updating me on her progress, Paul turned to his own concerns.

Divorced and the father of a teenage son and teenage daughter who lived with their mother, Paul excelled in sales at a large computer software firm. He had recently returned from a trip to Paris, which he had won for making 200 percent of quota. Paul was very busy, and by measures of position and salary, was considered successful.

Paul saw his life slowly strangulating in backlogs of mail, and he desperately sought therapy. This was Paul's first attempt to get help for his difficulty. Clearly, he had a procrastination problem (unlike his sister who had good time-management skills and was well-organized).

Paul was behind in returning phone calls, messages given to him by his secretary, e-mail, snail mail, voice mail, and doing items on his "To Do" list. "There's just not enough hours in the day," he wailed. "It's all piling up, I'm totally out of control." His sister urged him to consider seeing me when his problem led him to ignore her phone messages and mail.

## Paul's Problem Solved

"I keep promising myself: 'I'll catch up today, or maybe tomorrow—or at least over the weekend.'" But these promises had turned out to be as solid as any New Year's resolution. Paul was well aware of his own procrastination tricks.

"Has this always proved a problem?" I wondered.

"Well, yes," Paul admitted. "I've always had some amount of a procrastination problem. It seems to be growing recently, like a cancer. Surprisingly, as my procrastination gets worse, I seem to get more successful at work."

"Perhaps due to your success," I ventured, "You're getting more accounts, in addition to the extra accounts you now have to monitor. This, in turn, leads to more responsibilities and, consequently, to more communications. So the repercussions of your usual procrastination tendencies are multiplied by all the extra work generated by the additional accounts you're handling."

Paul agreed this made sense. Then we identified what he was telling himself about the mail that led to his procrastination. Some of his strongest demands were:

- Chores SHOULD take care of themselves and not plague me

- This involves focused concentration and close attention to boring detail. I SHOULDN'T have to call forth such effort

- It SHOULD be easy to stop what I'm absorbed in and face my mail

- There may be bills in the mail. I couldn't bear to face this and bring myself down from my level of current enjoyment. Mail SHOULDN'T bring unpleasant tidings

- I SHOULD not have negative repercussions as a result of not doing the mail

- I MUST do it perfectly and not handle anything incorrectly

- I MUST complete it all right now

Paul's misguided thinking was largely responsible for his self-destructive pattern. Contrary to the misconception that unhealthy emotions, such as anxiety, generate behavior, such as procrastination, irrational thinking does. Feelings are generated by thinking, and so are actions. If you change your views, you will thereby modify emotions and behaviors.

Consequently, I taught Paul to apply these steps to target his thinking:

1. Identify the irrational beliefs that lie at the heart of your procrastination.

2. Use Three Minute Exercises daily to reinforce more rational thinking. This will affect your actions and thereby help you to overcome your destructive procrastination.

3. Regularly practice the behavioral exercises in this chapter to help solidify and maintain your improvements.

## Paul's Three Minute Exercise

One of Paul's Three Minute Exercises looked like this:

A. (**A**ctivating event): I'm behind on making phone calls and on returning voice mail, e-mail, snail mail, phone messages given to me by my secretary, and on my "To Do" list.

B. (irrational **B**elief): These chores SHOULD take care of themselves and not plague me.

C. (emotional and behavioral **C**onsequences): Anxiety and procrastination.

D. (**D**isputing): Why SHOULD these chores take care of themselves and not plague me?

E. (**E**ffective new thinking): No reason exists that chores SHOULD take care of themselves and not plague me. Everyone has unpleasant tasks in their life. Since I'm not above the human condition, I can expect that I will too. This is uncomfortable, but never awful or terrible.

It's not the disagreeable nature of the chores that forces me to procrastinate, but rather it's my self-induced horror about this discomfort which creates my problem. If I ruthlessly push myself to face the messages, I'll feel uncomfortable briefly, but then I'll get it over with. However, if I continue to put it off, it will multiply and hang over my head forever. I have faced discomfort before and I've survived; I can face discomfort again and survive.

F. (new **F**eeling and behavior): Less anxiety. Pushing myself to attend to the messages and calls that have been accumulating.

## *Three Minute Judo: Make Inertia Work For You*

Like most emotional problems, unreasonable procrastination is best tackled by identifying your "musts" and disputing them, but there are also special techniques that have been found to be effective. A person who unreasonably procrastinates is usually aware that she is acting against her better judgment. There are useful stratagems to shift the balance in favor of the more rationally preferred course of action. It may take a little experimentation to find the techniques that work best for you.

If your problem is just one or a few important tasks that you keep putting off, try setting specific times each day or each week to devote to these tasks. Suppose, for example, that you've enrolled in a course in Italian and plan to possess a fair familiarity with spoken and written Italian by next year, when you visit your Uncle Giordano in Milan. Put exact times in your calendar to study for the course, refuse invitations that clash with those times, and in general, treat these appointments as you would the most serious appointments in your life.

The time you allocate to these sessions with the Italian course can be surprisingly brief, and can still be effective. Suppose that you study for the course for fifteen minutes at a fixed time each day. No one has decreed that you have to stop when the fifteen minutes are up! You can then elect to keep going for another three minutes, or even another fifteen minutes. Who knows? You may occasionally become engrossed and keep going for a couple of hours!

This illustrates the basic rationale of most anti-procrastination techniques: make inertia work FOR you. We all, in varying degrees, have a tendency to inertia; we all find it easier to continue what we're doing than to change gears and start doing something different. But once we have started doing that different thing, inertia begins to work in favor of sticking to it. The rationale is similar to that of judo (jujitsu) where the fighter learns ways to use his opponent's own weight to the opponent's disadvantage.

This principle can be taken to its ultimate in the Three Minute Procrastination Buster. In this technique, you simply decide that you will spend three minutes working on something, even though three minutes seems not worth doing. Suppose that you have been putting off an unpleasant chore for some time. Then you decide to give it three minutes.

"But," as some of my clients have protested, "I can't accomplish anything worthwhile in three minutes. What's the point?"

The point is to get started, and thereby get the force of inertia on your side. Even if it takes you four minutes to assemble the relevant file folders, so that you don't feel you can even begin the real job until you've spent four minutes preparing for it, just spend the three minutes all the same. But act the part convincingly: do everything just as if you were going to work at it for, let's say, the six hours you estimate the whole job will take.

"But what's the point of my spending only three minutes when I can't really begin until I'm four minutes into it? Isn't that irrational and purposeless behavior?"

No! In the first place, no one said you're rigidly locked into spending only three minutes. You just might choose to spend a fourth minute, or a fifth. (You don't have to, but you just might.) Secondly, that first three minutes of the four minutes' "preparation" is really beginning the job. If it sets up the job, it's part of the job. Thirdly, the appeal of the three minutes is that it's so little time that you may find it hard to begrudge. After all, you wouldn't begrudge spending three minutes helping a blind man you don't even know to get safely across the street. So why would you begrudge three minutes to help yourself, temporarily blinded by unreasonable procrastination, across the street to where you really want to go? Fourthly, the more you resist making yourself start on the distasteful task, the more you may intimidate yourself by thinking of the size of the entire task. In order to break that pattern of thinking, you chop that mammoth task into bite-sized pieces. You convince yourself in practice of the truth of the ancient Chinese proverb,

"Every journey of a thousand miles begins with a single step."

## *Getting Organized*

Some people are conspicuously organized: they meet deadlines while appearing unruffled, they cope with many difficult tasks, their desks or file cabinets look tidy. Other people are equally conspicuously poorly organized.

What is the connection between poor organization and unreasonable procrastination? It is not simple: well-organized people sometimes do practice unreasonable procrastination. Unreasonable procrastination afflicts the overwhelming majority of people (in varying degrees, of course). I have had as clients some dynamic sharpshooters who, it has turned out, were bothered by their unreasonable procrastination.

In some cases organizational skills are a matter of luck—a person just happened to learn useful skills from someone they worked with, for example. Norma was an administrator who had a lot of correspondence about many different matters to keep track of. For various reasons, a simple alphabetical or chronological system for all documents was not appropriate in this job. Norma was usually behind with filing, and frequently could not find a document within a reasonable time period.

Norma was very reluctant to start a new subject file. Because of her experience in a previous job, she thought this was a "big deal," which should not be entered on lightly. Then, for a week she helped out a colleague who had a similar job in a different department. Norma was surprised to find that this colleague, rather than spending time deliberating where a new document might be filed, would instantly start a new file. It so happened that in this particular job this was a better approach. Norma immediately applied this new technique in her own job and quickly eliminated most of her filing difficulties.

In other cases, however, unreasonable procrastination lies at the root of the failure to adopt good organizational methods. Lawrence was an office worker with numerous small and highly varied tasks. He was constantly in trouble because he did not complete some tasks soon enough, and when asked by his supervisor why not, he would explain that he had been working on some other task, which the supervisor usually judged to be of lower priority. Lawrence also found that he would not "get to" some tasks because they would "slip his mind."

Lawrence was provided with a "planner," a big day book with room to list all the tasks for each day. But Lawrence would stubbornly refuse to use the planner in the intended way. Instead of writing down all the tasks he hoped to get done on a particular day ahead of time, checking off those tasks as they were completed, he would write down the tasks for the first time after he had done them, and even then he would sometimes forget to write them down. So he never had a list he could look at of all the things competing for his time for the next few days. He could never confidently go to his supervisor and say: "I have completed x, y, and z. I plan to spend this afternoon on u and v, which seem to be most urgent. This means I will be a day late with w, which you told me you wanted by the end of today. I will be able to finish w tomorrow if nothing unexpected comes up. Is that okay?" Lawrence was resistant to changing his work habits because of his "musty" thinking.

As Lawrence saw it, writing out the tasks in advance took time away from performing the actual tasks. Like many people, he begrudged time spent "preparing" even though this would improve the efficiency of the "actual" work. He told himself that work MUST organize itself without planning, and that he MUST be able to choose at any time which of his tasks he would work on next, rather than following some predetermined schedule. In Lawrence's case, unreasonable procrastination was the major cause of his poor organization.

Prioritizing can be torpedoed by procrastination. Calvin made a list of six things he was behind with at work. He decided to give up a Sunday to spend ten hours in the office catching up on those six things. He went to the office, made himself a cup of coffee, and phoned a friend to chat for a few minutes. He noticed a few bits of minor correspondence from the previous Friday, and decided to spend "just a minute or two" getting them out of the way. When he had done that he noticed that an hour and a half had gone by. He made himself another cup of coffee and picked out one of the six tasks, the one which had some entertainment value for him. After staring at it for a while, he felt he couldn't really get going unless he first went to the bathroom. On his way back from the bathroom he noticed something that looked very interesting coming out of the fax machine, and he sat down to read it. Eleven hours after entering the office, it hit him that three of the six tasks were not touched, and only now did he clearly see that two of these three were the most urgent of the whole six, as judged by the seriousness of the consequences if they were not completed by 8:30 A.M. the following day.

Calvin's predicament resulted from three sources: underestimating the time required for tasks, being distracted by other less important things, and failing to do tasks in their true order of urgency. To combat tendencies like this, a variant of the No Future Regrets method can be useful. At the beginning of that Sunday, Calvin could have asked himself this question: "Suppose that two hours from now I am taken violently ill with food poisoning, or that the office is struck by lightning, all the computers crash, and I can do no more work for twenty-four hours. What will I think, looking back twenty-six hours from now, was the best possible use of these next two hours?" Having arrived at the answer, Calvin can work on that task first, even though he may believe that he will get to it eventually within the ten hours.

When poor organization arises from lack of organizational skills, it's a practical problem that can be tackled in various ways. There are books, tapes, and workshops on becoming more organized by planning one's time more effectively. But much can be learned simply by watching carefully those people who seem to be above-average in organizational skills, and copying the methods and procedures you observe them using.

## Sara's School Story

Sara, 19, was on the verge of getting expelled from college. She sat in my office mercilessly criticizing herself. As a consequence of months of delay, she was up late last night writing a paper to meet today's deadline. She finally completed it before dropping off for some scant hours of early morning sleep. Now she was wishing that she had started the paper months ago, far in advance of the due date, researching and writing a few pages each day.

Sara procrastinated on her studying, viewing it as too unpleasant to face. Ill-prepared for exams and term papers, she was doing poorly in her classes. This made school seem even more distasteful, leading to more procrastination. First, I taught her a Three Minute Exercise (similar to Paul's, above). Then we discussed a variety of behavioral tasks to combat procrastination.

I reminded Sara that what's done is done and can't be undone. Rather than thinking about what she SHOULD have done in the past, it was better to devise strategies for the future. I recommended that she start now, working on her next project, due in two months. The plan we devised comprised the following steps:

1. Select a project. Sara focused on writing her next paper.

2. Set a specific time each day to devote to it. 7:30 P.M. on weekdays, and 4:00 P.M. on weekends, seemed best. Sara gave herself Fridays off.

3. Spend a minimum of three minutes each day on it (the Three Minute Procrastination Buster). Sara found that this modest goal made it easier to sit down and get started.

4. After working for three minutes, evaluate if you wish to continue. Sara elected to continue working 80 to 90 percent of the time. On occasion, she devoted as much as forty-five minutes.

## *Give Yourself Rewards and Penalties*

As the end of the semester neared, so did Sara's final exam. She felt that she would not be adequately prepared unless she studied a minimum of two hours every day. However, she was skeptical about accomplishing this formidable task. Three Minute Penalties would provide immediate motivation, so I recommended this approach for Sara:

1. Select a project. For Sara, this consisted of studying for the final exam.

2. Decide on the specific days that you wish to set aside for your task, the duration of each work

period, and the starting time. Sara resolved to devote five days each week, with only Fridays and Saturdays off, work for two hours on each of these days, and begin after dinner at 7:30.

3. Select a penalty and a recipient and/or a reward. Sara chose to penalize herself one dollar for every minute less than the 120 minutes which she assigned herself to do. She would also levy a one dollar penalty for every minute after 7:30 that she began to work. She opted to send the money to her least favorite cause: the campaign fund of a politician she loathed. Her reward for full compliance that day would be a twenty-minute bubble bath before going to bed.

4. Immediately levy the penalty for noncompliance. If this evening Sara began studying at 7:35, for example, her penalty would be five dollars. If, in addition, she studied for only 90—rather than 120—minutes, she would owe an additional $30. She consequently would send a total of $35 to her most hated politician's campaign fund, immediately after ending the evening's studying.

Sara understood the procedure, and it made sense to her. However, she had one objection:

"I would hate to send that slimy crook any money. In fact, I don't know if I could get myself to do it," she confessed.

"To make sure that you do," I suggested, "when you arrive home tonight, immediately address and stamp an envelope to that slimy crook's campaign. Then write a check, leaving only the amount blank, and put it in the envelope. Now, if the time comes to pay a penalty, all it will take is filling out the amount on the check and then putting it in the mail," I explained.

"I guess that would increase the likelihood of my sending it."

"If this still seems like an impossible task, bring the stamped, addressed envelope and check to me. Should you slip up on the studying, tell me how much you owe the slimy crook. I'll fill in that amount and mail it for you."

"Hmm, I see. Thanks." Sara's momentary frown relaxed into a smile.

"But since you find the penalty so odious, don't forget the simple trick which will ensure that you never send the slimy crook one red cent."

"And that is?"

"That is: Simply study for two hours beginning at 7:30 P.M., every night, without fail!"

Sara grinned.

## Premack's Principle

Sara would sometimes lull herself into procrastinating—a moment at a time—until the entire day would slip by. She would think: "I'll just have a cup of coffee, then I'll buckle down." After the coffee, she might say: "Now's a good time to phone my friend Jennie, before she leaves for class. I'll just chat with her for a minute." After the 60-minute chat, it was "time to check the mail," and so on. This chain of rationalizations might continue until she finally decided that it was time to go to bed, and therefore it was too late, and she was too tired to do any work. I recognized this as an opportunity to apply Premack's Principle, formulated by psychologist David Premack, which states: A higher frequency behavior can reinforce a lower frequency behavior.

Suppose brewing yourself a cup of coffee is something you do often and easily (a higher frequency behavior). Suppose further, that vacuuming your living room rug is something you do rarely and with difficulty (a lower frequency behavior).

To implement Premack's Principle, don't allow yourself to do the higher frequency behavior (making yourself a cup of coffee) until you've done the lower frequency behavior (vacuuming the rug). Sara committed herself to two hours of school work five days each week. She would allow herself a cup of coffee after she put in thirty minutes of studying, and not allow herself to phone a friend (another high frequency behavior) until after she completed the entire two hours.

## *Three Minute Wake-up Imagery*

It's 7:00 A.M. on Monday. Sara's clock radio automatically goes on, blaring the morning news. She stirs from under the warm covers. Dazed and only partially emerging from a deep sleep, she hits the clock's "off" button. She then promptly falls back to sleep. Two hours later, Sara awakes unassisted, glances at the time and frantically makes a beeline for the shower. This was a common pattern for her, especially on Monday mornings.

I gave Sara two suggestions: 1) retire earlier, and 2) use three minute wake-up imagery. These are the instructions for the latter: Every night, before getting into bed, vividly picture the following:

The clock strikes 7:00 A.M. You spring out of bed and plunge into the shower. While imagining this, strongly repeat to yourself: "No excuses and no debates—as soon as the clock strikes 7:00 A.M. I will spring out of bed and rush into the shower, come hell or high water." Do this for three minutes, repeating the imagery in your head, and restating the motivational statement.

Sara discovered that when she practiced this *Wake-Up Imagery*, it worked. Sometimes when she neglected to practice the imagery, she succeeded nevertheless in getting up on time. However, after failing to practice it for several consecutive nights, she would sometimes oversleep, and this reminded her to return to the exercise.

# 7

## *Depression: To Hell and Back*

*The mind is its own place, and in itself can make a Heav'n of Hell, a Hell of Heav'n.*
—JOHN MILTON (1608–1674)

If you saw someone repeatedly hitting himself with a hammer, you would probably assume that, for some mysterious reason, he wanted to hurt himself. If this person complained bitterly that he was covered with painful bruises and would do anything to escape from the torment, you might point out to him that he could accomplish this very easily: all he has to do is stop hitting himself.

Now suppose that this person takes your advice and stops hitting himself with the hammer. And two minutes later, he says: "Well, I still feel lousy. My bruises are still giving me Hell. That didn't seem to work, and I really have a strong urge to start hitting myself again, so that's what I'll do."

If you believed that this person was in earnest, you would explain to him that it takes time for the bruises to go away. But you might also explain that he doesn't really need to keep hitting himself. He doesn't gain anything by it, so he might as well stop, even though this apparently requires an effort.

In reality, we do not often observe such ridiculous behavior. If you hit yourself with a hammer, it hurts physically. The pain is so sharp and immediate that you can hardly fail to notice the connection between the hammer blows and the pain. You would therefore be unlikely to get into the habit of hitting yourself with a hammer without noticing that you were doing so.

It's not so obvious to people that when they're depressed it's directly caused by their "musty" thinking. If you tell yourself you're a worthless clod, there is no piercing, obvious warning that impels you to stop thinking like that. So you may get into the habit of telling yourself this sort of thing. You may even develop this habit without noticing it.

Then, one day, you may start to experience the equivalent of bruises and broken bones. You become aware that you are suffering from depression. And you may refuse to believe that you have brought the depression upon yourself by your "musty" thinking.

## To Be or Not to Be Depressed

Bruce had the appearance of a stage Hamlet, his black turtleneck shirt, black denims, and black shoes and socks contrasting starkly with his shock of wavy blond hair, ashen complexion, and pale mustache.

Although he had taken acting courses, Bruce had been a machine shop foreman for the past two years. He had never been married yet had a five-year-old son, Timmy, from a previous living-together relationship. Both he and Timmy were currently sharing an apartment with Bruce's father and step-mother who were recent immigrants from Latvia. They spoke little English and so they depended on Bruce, who was resourceful and bright, to make many of their decisions.

Bruce had been depressed as far back as he could remember. He would get particularly depressed at times "for no apparent reason" and have difficulty sleeping and concentrating. He sometimes felt isolated and would "put walls up and not let people get close." At other times, he got depressed about not having a relationship with his biological mother (he hadn't seen her for a year and a half), and at work he felt distant from his co-workers and was perfectionistic about his performance.

"But the thing that really gets me down the most," he explained in his resonant actor's voice, "is that I'm incapable of forming a lasting relationship with a woman. In my life, I have had sex with thirty-seven women, and started relationships with eleven of them. I would really like to settle down, but I'm almost thirty, and it will soon be too late."

Six years earlier he had lived with Monique for twelve months. Although they both had Timmy, Monique's severe emotional problems made the relationship very difficult for Bruce. His most recent relationship had ended after five weeks. In response to my queries about why it had terminated, he shrugged and said only: "I don't know what happened." He seemed genuinely mystified.

We delved further into the details of his past relationships. It soon became apparent that Bruce had a tendency to deify women and quickly to fall hopelessly in love with them. Then he would typically pursue them even as their major psychological problems emerged. We discussed why he did not end these relationships sooner, what he could do about it, and how he could identify and pursue healthier relationships.

Here are some of the thoughts that Bruce had been thinking for years:

- I MUST not hurt her, and if I do I'm a total louse

- I SHOULD have had a fulfilling relationship by now, and at the age of twenty-nine it will soon be too late. I MUST have a relationship right now or else I'm a cipher

- I SHOULD be like everyone else; since they're all passionately involved in rewarding relationships and I'm not, this lack shows what a rotten person I am. I MUST always have someone around and I can't stand to be alone and lonely. I MUST be accepted by someone I care about and because I'm not I'm a pitiable slob

- I MUST know why it didn't work out, or else I'll never have a satisfactory relationship

- I SHOULDN'T have so many failed relationships and because I have had them, I'm destined to always fail in relationships.

## *The Great Debate*

These "musts," these unreasonable demands upon himself, lay at the root of his depression, insomnia, and isolation. I taught Bruce how to combat these "musty" thoughts with the Three Minute Exercise, but when I saw him next time, he told me that he had "tried the exercise, but it didn't work."

When a client tells me this, it usually turns out that the client hasn't really tried the exercise, but Bruce had fully written out Three Minute Exercises to show me, and he was disappointed that he had apparently made no progress.

The problem was that when he wrote out stage E ("Effective new thinking"), he didn't really find it convincing. For example, he attempted to dispute the irrational belief (B) "I MUST have a relationship right now, and if I don't, I never will." At D he asked: "Where is the evidence I MUST have this relationship right now, or else I never will?" At E he wrote: "It would be lovely to have a relationship right now, but there's no 'must' about it, and it's entirely possible that I will not start a relationship for a year or more, and will then start one."

But as he wrote this, a voice in the back of his head would comment: "Who are you kidding? You know very well that the kind of bright, attractive, stable woman you're looking for would never be interested in a lowlife like you!" At that point he was stymied.

Our beliefs tend to hang together consistently. One belief may be supported by other beliefs, and these in turn by yet other beliefs. The specific belief we're trying to change may be very resistant, because it is strongly implied by other beliefs that we have done nothing to challenge. The solution is to challenge all the beliefs that lead to irrational demands, and this means engaging in debate.

I recommended to Bruce the technique I call *Debating Until You Win.* The way this works is that every time you come up with some "reason" for clinging to your old "musty" thoughts, you challenge that "reason." You talk back to that little voice. You can win the argument, because that little voice hasn't thought deeply or reflected critically—it merely expresses unexamined, unscientific notions you have been harboring for years.

It's helpful to commit the debate to paper, so that you can clearly see that you have a good answer to anything the "musty" voice might say. This is how such a debate might look:

> MUSTY VOICE: I MUST have a relationship right now, and because I don't, I never will.
> CLEAR-THINKING VOICE: It would be lovely to have a relationship right now, but there's no 'must' about it, and it's entirely possible that I will not start

a relationship for a year or more, and will then start one.

MUSTY VOICE: Who are you kidding? You know very well that the kind of bright, attractive, stable woman you're looking for would never be interested in a lowlife like you!

CLEAR-THINKING VOICE: You're claiming two things: 1. By calling me a "lowlife" you're saying I'm no good. 2. You're also saying I'm doomed to failure. Can you prove either of these claims?

MUSTY VOICE: You've always failed at this so far! You've never had a long-term satisfying relationship. There's the proof! You never will! Give up!

CLEAR-THINKING VOICE: It quite frequently happens that people succeed at things after failing for years. So "have not" (past tense) doesn't prove "will not" (future tense).

MUSTY VOICE: But in your case you "haven't" had a successful relationship because no one decent would want to have a relationship with you!

CLEAR-THINKING VOICE: You're practicing fortune-telling without a crystal ball! Where's your proof? The more women I meet, the better my chances of connecting with someone that's for me. So I plan to start meeting them.

MUSTY VOICE: That's not good enough! You MUST have a relationship right now.

CLEAR-THINKING VOICE: Reality is what it is, not what I think it MUST be. The reality is that I don't have a relationship right now. Tough! A relationship sometime in the future is better than no relationship ever, so let's think about what's feasible—a future relationship. The first step toward this goal is to cease moaning about not having a relationship now, and instead take steps to make it more likely I will have a relationship some time.

Moreover, the fact that I've never yet had the solid type of relationship that I would like doesn't make me a worm or a lowlife. If I have some traits that cause problems in relationships, I can probably figure out what these are and start to improve them. And I'm more likely to do that by meeting women so that I can get practice relating to them.

## A Sparring Partner

To help Bruce develop his skills in these debates, I had oral debates with him in which I played the part of the Musty Voice and he played the Clear-Thinking Voice. Given the stimulus of a contest with another person, Bruce quickly became alert to my fallacious "musty" ploys, and was able to refute them with ease. I am happy to report that, before long, he was able to administer the KO in Round One every time.

Ten months after ending therapy, Bruce wrote to me. His feelings of depression were now rare and brief. He had met a woman who was more emotionally stable than any of his previous girlfriends, and they were considering marriage when she finished business school in four months. He thanked me and wrote: "At times I can still hear your voice in the back of my head, saying 'Past failure doesn't *cause* future failure.' "

## Myths About Depression and Relationships

A common misconception is that depression always means lethargy, so that people who are energetic and active cannot be depressed. But this is to confuse one possible consequence of depression with depression itself. Some depressed people are very hard-working and conscientious, and some, like Bruce, have had lots of relationships.

Another misconception, fostered by the old post-Freudian style of psychotherapy, is that people who repeatedly have failed relationships "unconsciously" seek out those partners who will be bad for them. But there is a simpler explanation that seems to fit the facts better.

We are not suited for long-term relationships with many of the individuals we date. Most people recognize this and terminate unpromising relationships at an early stage, many almost before they have begun. By contrast, people with many failed relationships, like Bruce, are inclined to persist with unpromising relationships, because of unrealistic, "musty" thinking. They may, for example, think "I MUST avoid discomfort, therefore I couldn't face the prospect of telling my partner it's over." Or: "If the relationship isn't perfect (the way it SHOULD be) it's my fault, so I will never find anyone who'd be any better."

Other people bring to their relationships such unrealistic assumptions that they are bound to be disappointed. They may think: "A good relationship will be continually easy, pleasurable, and hassle-free. If my present relationship isn't like that, then it's unworkable."

## *Nursed Back to Health*

One of the most common obstacles to overcoming depression is that sufferers insist on a dramatic, immediate improvement. If this doesn't happen, they start to think, "It's hopeless; nothing will do any good." This applies to all emotional problems, but is particularly marked with depression.

At 31, glowing in soft pink designer sweats, Carla looked as if she had just stepped out of a health and fitness magazine. She was head nurse at a Fortune 500 firm; evenings and weekends she taught yoga at a health club.

Carla described herself as "terribly depressed" and had begun to entertain thoughts of suicide. She likened her marriage of four years to a yo-yo: "Whenever things start to go well, a crisis hits big time." She felt insecure about her career, all the more since rumors of downsizing had begun circulating at work.

After I had helped her to separate her practical and emotional problems and to practice Three Minute Exercises to combat her "musty" thinking, she became impatient and started telling herself: "I SHOULD be entirely cured of depression by now. Since I'm not, I've accomplished nothing. Nothing works. I give up."

## Day by Day

But as with learning a musical instrument, daily progress is often imperceptible. Since Carla found it hard to believe she really was making progress, I recommended *Daily Mood Ratings.* Every night, Carla would estimate just how depressed she had been that day, on a scale from 0 to 100 percent. She would later enter the score on a chart. For a ten-week period, her chart looked like this:

|           | Week #1 | Week #2 | Week #3 | Week #4 | Week #5 |
|-----------|---------|---------|---------|---------|---------|
| **Tuesday**   | 60% | 80% | 50% | 60% | 50% |
| **Wednesday** | 80% | 80% | 80% | 50% | 40% |
| **Thursday**  | 70% | 60% | 80% | 70% | 30% |

| Friday | 60% | 50% | 60% | 40% | 50% |
|--------|-----|-----|-----|-----|-----|
| Saturday | 60% | 70% | 40% | 60% | 50% |
| Sunday | 90% | 70% | 70% | 60% | 60% |
| Monday | 80% | 60% | 60% | 40% | 40% |

| | Week #6 | Week #7 | Week #8 | Week #9 | Week #10 |
|--------|---------|---------|---------|---------|----------|
| Tuesday | 50% | 40% | 50% | 30% | 0% |
| Wednesday | 40% | 40% | 40% | 10% | 0% |
| Thursday | 40% | 40% | 20% | 0% | 0% |
| Friday | 10% | 20% | 20% | 0% | 0% |
| Saturday | 30% | 30% | 0% | 0% | 0% |
| Sunday | 60% | 50% | 40% | 30% | 20% |
| Monday | 40% | 30% | 30% | 10% | 10% |

During the first few weeks she frequently scored 70 and 80 percent, indicating that she was quite depressed. However, as she did her daily Three Minute Exercises, relentlessly disputed her "musty" thinking, and pushed herself to face discomfort, her mood slowly lifted. After two months (it seemed like a lifetime to Carla) she was feeling only mildly depressed only some of the time, and then only infrequently.

Carla succeeded in holding her depression at bay and living a fuller life. She later came back to me, bringing her husband, to work on their "yo-yo" marriage.

## *Stop Depressing Yourself*

Depression can be mild or severe. The depressed person feels worthless, helpless, and hopeless; the severely depressed person sees everyday life as a living Hell. Gloom and despair seem to pervade every waking moment, and preoccupation with suicide is common, sometimes leading to actual suicide. Severe depression restricts the capacity to enjoy life—the sufferer finds that things she used to really enjoy and look forward to, like a certain kind of food or music, no longer thrill or inspire. Everything seems flat and stale.

Many people who have suffered severe depression for years report that they would far rather undergo serious physical pain than the extreme mental anguish of depression. Some sufferers say, and sincerely believe, that they would do *anything* to escape depression.

But there is something they can do—they can stop depressing themselves. This is easier said than done, but it *can* be done. It will very likely do little good, however, for the sufferer to take the obvious commonsense approach of focusing his mind on cheerful topics. If, for instance, the sufferer keeps telling himself he is a worthless clod, he *believes* that he is a worthless clod, and this belief generates his depression. Making an effort to "put on a happy face" does nothing to combat this entrenched belief. It is more effective to challenge that false belief, root it out, and replace it with a more rational belief using Three Minute Exercises.

Circumstances by themselves have no power to depress you. No matter how extreme the misfortune a person faces, the objective facts in that person's environment don't by themselves cause emotional upset. There are numerous examples showing the power of the mind to remain composed under any circumstances. Consider a few of them:

Ingrid Bergman, the three-time Academy Award winner and star of the classic movie "Casablanca," said of her terminal cancer: "I have accepted it, and will make the most of what's left of my life while I can. Cancer victims who don't accept their fate, who don't learn to live with it, will only destroy what little time they have left."

Bergman matter-of-factly accepted her pain-filled day-to-day existence and her imminent death. She went on to give an outstanding performance in her final movie on the life of Golda Meir.

David Hume, the great Scottish philosopher who died in 1776, knew his death was coming soon and announced the fact in a good-humored short autobiography written four months before his demise. His doctor reported that at the end of his life, though very weak, he was "quite free from anxiety, impatience, or low spirits."

True, the individuals in these examples were faced with nothing worse than physical deterioration followed by death. Can people avoid being upset when they're in *real* trouble? What's the worst situation imaginable? Some would suggest being an inmate in a Nazi concentration camp—physically abused and always under the threat of death. Yet we know from reports of camp survivors that inmates in the same circumstances did not all respond in the same way. Some became anxious, depressed, frantic, or suicidal. Others behaved utterly differently, refusing to upset themselves needlessly about their plight. For evidence see *Man's Search for Meaning* by Victor Frankl.

## Pamela's Self-Pity Party

Pamela, a 26-year-old counselor at a methadone day-treatment facility, had a gaunt, underweight appearance, which she was quick to attribute to "job stress." She wore a southwestern-design vest with a collarless shirt and black jeans. Her quick smile vanished within a split second, to be replaced by a gloomy stare.

Although not highly paid, Pamela, who lived with her lesbian partner Megan and their two young children, contributed most of the household income. She was vocally dissatisfied with her work, yet after three years was still at the same job. "The work is meaningless, the pay isn't much to live on, the hours are too long, and the prospects are zilch," she told me. Pamela had completed two years of college and declared, unconvincingly: "One day I plan to go back and study computer science."

Years of worsening depression finally motivated her to seek therapy. She readily made herself depressed about daily inconveniences. Over the last month these included catching the flu, an increasing client load at work, some of these clients getting worse, one of the kids crying most of the night, fights with Megan over whether Pamela should do more with the children, and a flat tire while driving home from work one evening.

Pamela irritably described her previous day. After breakfast she was about to leave home and go to work. Unfortunately, she couldn't find her car keys. She frantically searched her house—inside pockets, under tables, chairs, and couches, and in and around the car—all to no avail. She finally gave up in disgust and hastily called a taxi to take her to the train station. As luck would have it, just as the cab pulled into the station, Pamela heard her train pulling out. She ultimately arrived at work forty minutes late, wallowing in self-pity. When her boss criticized her for her lateness, she felt utterly defeated.

I explained to Pamela that she had two different types of problems. The series of inconveniences were *Practical* Problems, whereas her depression was a self-created and gratuitous *Emotional* Problem.

Pamela quickly conceded that the Practical Problems, though troublesome, were not what was really upsetting her. Rather, she soon acknowledged, it was her unrealistic view, specifically, "Life MUST not give me these headaches or else all is hopeless," that caused her upset. She saw, also, that by repeating this thought to himself whenever faced with unpleasant or unfair situations, she re-indoctrinated herself, thereby maintaining her disturbance.

## *Pamela's Three Minute Exercise*

A. (**A**ctivating event): Today I had many hassles: I lost my keys, I missed my train, and the boss unfairly criticized me.

B. (irrational **B**elief): Life MUST not give me these headaches or else all is hopeless.

C. (emotional **C**onsequences): Depression, self-pity.

D. (**D**isputing): What is the evidence life MUST not give me enormous headaches?

E. (**E**ffective new thinking): There is simply *no* evidence demonstrating that life MUST not give me such nuisances. Life often consists of one hassle after another. Too bad! It's not the inconveniences themselves, but rather my catastrophizing about them that depresses me.

Hassles are just that—hassles, never horrors. Since I'm not a privileged super-being, the universe will not protect me from troubles. I can considerably enjoy life with them, even if they increase. By pushing myself, I can still accomplish things while hassled. I've always had hassles, I always will, and no reason exists why I MUST not.

Simply because it would be lovely if life did not give me inconveniences does not mean it MUST not. It's sad that reality gives me these difficulties, but hardly the end of the world. I can view hassles as blocks to be overcome. Many will prove to be challenging and stimulating, rather than tragedies.

I'm an imperfect human being, so I will be inefficient sometimes and lose my keys or otherwise create problems for myself. I can greatly enjoy life even with this inefficient tendency, as long as I refuse to moan and groan about it.

F. (new **F**eeling): Concern rather than depression and self-pity about life's nuisances.

## *Three Second Knockouts*

At this juncture, I decided the technique of the *Three Second Knockout* would be helpful for Pamela. Here, you devise a pithy, dramatic statement that challenges and contradicts a major irrational belief you're fighting. Throughout the day, when your mind is not otherwise engaged, meaningfully and persuasively say the "knockout" statement to yourself. The repetition will help reinforce the statement, etching it into your brain. Then, when "musty" thoughts appear, they can be quickly clobbered.

For example, in Pamela's case we devised the "knockout" statement, "If I have hassles, I have hassles. Too damn bad!" I instructed her to repeat this "knockout" statement to herself throughout the day. To help motivate and focus her we set up a goal—one hundred repetitions each day. We got the "knockout" statement going around in her head so that it would eventually become part of the way she viewed hassles.

Pamela reported that after hundreds of repetitions this particular phrase began to get clichéd and stale. So we devised another to use for variety: "Hassles are only hassles, NEVER horrors!" For an entire day she would use one or the other "knockout" statement, whichever seemed more meaningful to her at the time. Alternating between the two solved the problem of staleness.

Pamela found the Knockout technique particularly helpful. She got to the point where, as a result of using the Knockout statements, she would stop upsetting herself about inconveniences for weeks. But eventually, for no apparent reason, she would start depressing herself all over again.

We discovered the explanation. Once Pamela began accepting hassles more gracefully, she would stop using the Knockout technique. She did so on the grounds that she was finally cured, once and for all. But soon her "musts" would slowly creep back into her head, and she would become depressed again. So we developed a pre-emptive strike to practice when things were going *well*: "Life *will* consist of one hassle after another, and it *should!"*

## Pamela's Progress

One morning, about a year after Pamela had completed therapy, I was pleasantly surprised to receive a phone call from her. She happily informed me that her depression was largely gone. On the one or two occasions that it had started to emerge, she had practiced her Three Minute Exercises and Three Second Knockouts and soon vanquished it.

Moreover, Pamela was applying to college to follow through on her dream to study computer science. She had some money saved and felt ready to face the disruptions of a major career change. She asked if I would write a reference for her. I said I would be delighted.

# 8

## *Overeating and Smoking: It's All in Your Head*

*The very nature of man impels him to satisfy his desires with the least possible pain.*
—FRÉDÉRIC BASTIAT (1801–1850)

They say that inside every fat person there's a thin person fighting to get out. In Suzie's case, the thin person appeared to be losing the struggle. At 5'4" Suzie felt she ought to be 130 lbs, but was actually closer to 160.

Just about to turn 20, Suzie looked older. She had deep eyes and smooth chestnut hair beneath her floppy leghorn hat, and wore a silk print dress with an enormous string of crystal beads. She had a lively manner and was ready to laugh, but seemed imprisoned by her excess fat. She was disheartened. "I've tried dozens of diets over the last five years, and I work out four times a week, but I can't seem to lose weight consistently, and I'm heavier now than I was a year ago."

When Suzie told me her exercise regimen, I felt exhausted just listening to it. She was at the gym never less than four evenings a week; for the first 30 minutes she vigorously pedaled an exercise bike, followed by an even more demanding 60-minute aerobics class. Yet she remained overweight.

## *The Solution to Suzie's Puzzle*

Suzie was sincerely mystified as to why she "could not" manage to reduce. On one level, the answer was obvious: She was absorbing enough excess calories to outweigh the effects of her exercise. Suzie immediately confirmed that she often yielded to impulsive temptations to drink too much alcohol and to snack on high-calorie foods. So the real puzzle was: How can someone with the drive and determination to stick to a grueling exercise program fail to control her eating and drinking habits? The answer is that addictions arise from addictive thinking. On her first visit I gave Suzie a personality questionnaire, which confirmed my immediate guess. The test involved circling one of the three words "OFTEN," "SOMETIMES," or "SELDOM" after each of 50 statements. Suzie indicated "OFTEN" for these statements:

- I feel upset when things proceed slowly and can't be settled quickly

- I feel upset about life's inconveniences or frustrations

- I feel quite angry when someone keeps me waiting

- I feel very sorry for myself when things are rough

- I feel unable to persist at things I start, especially when the going gets hard

- I feel unexcited and bored about most things

## Low Frustration Tolerance

Suzie was suffering from *Low Frustration Tolerance,* a very common type of "musty" thinking, which lies at the root of the great majority of overeating problems and other addictions.

Low Frustration Tolerance arises from the third "must," the belief that life MUST be fair, easy, well-ordered, comfortable, exciting, pleasurable, interesting, or hassle-free. In any situation where life does not conform to such demands, the addict compulsively looks for a quick escape from these "unbearable" circumstances.

Suzie told me more about her problems. She was moody and often depressed about weight, friends, and boy-friends. She had broken up with Sammy a year earlier, but continued to see him off and on. (She had a demand about this situation: "I MUST know for sure if it's on or off with Sammy.")

## The Power of Negative Thinking

A specific technique has often been found effective in undermining Low Frustration Tolerance and thereby curing addictive thinking. This method is to maintain a clear and constant awareness of the *disadvantages* of any particular behavior or outlook. I explained the idea to Suzie:

"Whenever you do anything that is under your voluntary control, even getting out of bed in the morning, all the way to getting into bed at night, you make the decision to do it. And every decision largely consists of a weighing of benefits against costs, or advantages against disadvantages.

"When you get up in the morning, you're demonstrating that at that moment you believe the advantages of arising outweigh the disadvantages (skipping breakfast, rushing to work, arriving late, and so on). If you had decided that the disadvantages of getting out of bed were greater, then you would have stayed in bed. This process—often operating semi-automatically—repeats itself throughout the day in making large and small decisions.

"It's exactly the same with your eating or overeating. Whenever you choose to eat pizza, or any other high fat food, it's because you've decided, for the moment, that the advantages of doing so outweigh the disadvantages. Just before making such a decision, you might be thinking something like: 'This pizza is fattening (disadvantage 1), but it tastes so delicious (advantage 1), I'll feel so good (advantage 2), I HAVE TO crave it (advantage 3), and I won't really gain weight because I'll diet later (discounting disadvantage 1).'

"If you can convince yourself that the calculation is reasonable and that the advantages outweigh the disadvantages, you will indulge. If we can get you to realize, strongly and clearly in such situations, that the disadvantages outweigh the advantages, then you will reject the pizza."

## *Harnessing the Power*

How did I get Suzie to remain convinced, at the moment of temptation, that the disadvantages outweighed the advantages? Practice, repetition, and reinforcement. Here are some of the most effective techniques:

1. *List the disadvantages.* I asked Suzie to make a detailed and extensive list of the disadvantages of eating pizza. She came up with over 30 items, including:

- It's fattening

- I feel guilty afterwards

- I could spend the money on something else

- I'm more likely to become depressed

- I'll be less healthy

- It adds to my difficulty fitting into clothes

The longer the list, the more powerful the technique, even if some items are repetitive. (Suzie wrote: "I'll be less healthy," "It will raise my cholesterol level," and "I'll be more susceptible to some diseases.")

2. *Vividly read through the disadvantages.* I advised Suzie to read through the list of disadvantages every day, and to spend some time dwelling on each item at its worst. For "It's fattening," she would picture herself eating while getting fatter and fatter until she became hugely obese, then getting fatter still, and becoming increasingly uncomfortable because of her extra weight.

3. *Practice imagining the disadvantages.* Next, I asked Suzie to adopt the habit of vividly reminding herself of the disadvantages of compulsive eating, in situations where it was impracticable to refer to the list. When driving, while preparing or eating dinner, when walking down the street, waiting in line or on hold, she would vividly picture one of the disadvantages of pigging out.

Suzie liked to listen to music tapes while driving. We decided that when she first got into the car, she would spend a few minutes vividly imagining some of the disadvantages of overeating, before she allowed herself to put on a tape.

4. *Referenting.* I also explained to Suzie the principle of "referenting." Whenever she thought of junk food, either spontaneously or in response to some external stimulus such as seeing an advertisement or the aroma of food, then she would immediately concentrate on some of the disadvantages on her list.

The first day Suzie began to use referenting, she was walking past a pizza parlor and looked in at the pizzas. She started to think about the tasty and pleasurable aspects of pizza, but quickly noticed the way her thoughts were going, and deliberately reminded herself: "Fattening . . . unhealthy . . . feeling regret afterwards... I won't look good ...won't fit into my clothes ..."

Consistent use of referenting caused Suzie to have a heightened and more immediate awareness of the disadvantages of overeating, so that the temptation to pig out became easier to overcome.

Meanwhile, Suzie employed Three Minute Exercises to challenge and topple her "musts." Some of these "musts" were:

- The pounds MUST come off quickly

- Life SHOULD be more fun

- I MUST be thinner, or else I'm less of a person

If I start to feel bored or dissatisfied, I MUST feel better right away Suzie began to control her eating better, to feel better, and to drink less.

## Suzie's Setback

I was surprised and curious when Suzie arrived for her fourth session with a down-in-the-dumps air about her.

"Gee, I really blew it," she announced, as she flopped down into the chair dejectedly.

"In what way?"

"Well, let's see. I left here on Thursday night, went straight home, and watched some TV. All I had was an apple, a cup of decaf, and some popcorn. Oh yeah, some skim milk in the decaf, and that's it."

"Any butter, oil, or cheese on that popcorn?"

"No, I just got a hot air popper. All I put on was a pinch of salt."

"Okay. Great."

"Then Friday and Saturday went okay. Saturday, I went to a club with Sammy, but I didn't have any beer or wine. Sunday, I had coffee with toast and a grapefruit, and tuna salad for dinner."

"Sounds like an excellent week diet-wise, so far."

"Yeah, I thought I was in control. But I don't know what happened on Monday night. I was feeling kind of crummy about work. I went out for lunch and had a salad bar. But I started thinking about the cherry pie on display, and I was feeling very low and thought I'd have just a little pie to feel better. So I got one slice."

"Uh-oh," I said, with a tone of mock dismay.

"Well, when I slipped up like this the time before, I just reminded myself, as you told me: 'So I had a setback. Too bad! That's to be expected. I'll just get right back on track.' And I just snapped out of it, and it was no big deal. But this time, after the cherry pie, I was still feeling lousy, so I got another piece. So then I figured I'd really blown it, and I had cookies throughout the afternoon until I left work. Now I'm doing better again, I guess, but I'm still depressed about Monday."

"It sounds as if you basically did quite okay this week, except for that isolated cherry pie and cookies incident. But let's look a little closer at what went on in your head. You slipped up with the pie, which was natural.

"Yes. But the time before I recovered quickly— immediately after the slip-up."

"Right. But what were you telling yourself this time after you finished the first piece of cherry pie?"

"I don't know. I think I was comparing my last quick recovery to this time."

"And was the 'must': 'I MUST recover quickly...'?"

"Yeah, that was it."

"So you were telling yourself: 'Last time I immediately felt determined to get back on track, but now I'm still feeling lousy, I haven't recovered, and therefore I'm a hopeless failure. So I'll just be fat for the rest of my life.'"

"That's it! I felt I MUST recover quickly, just like the time before."

## Back On Track

I asked Suzie to write at the top of a page: "I MUST recover quickly, as I did last time." Then, I helped her to list all the reasons why this "must" was false. We came up with 14 of them:

1. No law carved in stone states that I MUST.

2.  It's typically human and understandable that I would upset myself about a setback.

3.  I can recover slowly.

4.  It's just a hassle, not a horror.

5.  I'm not worthless because I screw up.

6.  If I don't recover quickly, I can learn from my mistakes and eventually do better at recovering.

7.  Recovering slowly means that success takes longer. It doesn't mean total failure.

8.  One failure doesn't mean total failure, or that I'll never succeed.

9.  This just means I had better work harder at it next time.

10. This assumes that I MUST be thin—but, although I would like to be thin, I don't HAVE to be.

11. I can stand slow recoveries, although I don't like them.

12. Reality is reality, not what I think it MUST be.

13. If I pressure myself to always recover quickly, that will tend to make it more difficult to do so.

14. Being an imperfect human, like all humans, I will sometimes act imperfectly.

I gave Suzie the assignment of reading this list through thoughtfully three times a day for a month. She found this very helpful. She stopped putting pressure on herself to recover quickly from her overeating lapses, and then (paradoxical though it may seem) she had quicker recoveries and fewer relapses.

### Sunday's Blues

On one visit, Suzie reported she had eaten some junk food the previous Sunday but didn't know why. I asked her to tell me about her day.

"Sunday was a rather unstructured day, as usual. I just sat around lazily having breakfast, looking through the paper, and chatting aimlessly with my mom and sister. Sammy called and a friend called. Soon it was early afternoon. It was getting too late to invite Mazie to go to the beach or ask Cheryl to go shopping. I began to think about work on Monday. Then I started eating."

Eating junk food was the C. After I had tracked down some of Suzie's A's, it soon became clear what her B's were: "Sunday SHOULD be more exciting. I SHOULD have planned my day earlier. Weekends SHOULDN'T be so short. I MUSTN'T be bored. I SHOULDN'T have to go back to work tomorrow."

"Yes," said Suzie. "Now I see why I ate all that junk food on Sunday." As sometimes happens, just the insight into her demands helped her to uproot them.

### Sour Grapes

At another session, Suzie said that she overate because she didn't really care about dieting. If she got fat, what did it matter?

This is a common reaction when people begin to notice that their "musts" are irrational and unwarranted. They skip to the contrary view, that what they want isn't important at all. I explained to Suzie that telling herself "it doesn't matter" is a rationalization, an excuse she gives herself, so that she can pursue a different demand.

"Like what demand," asked Suzie.

134

"Like 'I GOTTA have the food!' " I responded.

Behind Suzie's rationalization ("I don't care about overeating—being thin is of no importance") lay these "musts":

- I SHOULD have been born thin

- Life SHOULDN'T be so unfair

- I SHOULD be able to eat whatever I want (without any consequences I dislike)

- Controlling my eating SHOULD be easy

Suzie did many Three Minute Exercises on her "musts." She came to accept herself with her setbacks, to accept that resisting her gustatory cravings was uncomfortable but bearable, and to acknowledge that being thin was an important preference but not an absolute demand. The pounds began to come off, and she was down to her ideal weight within six months. Just recently, three years later, I happened to see her again, and she was happily maintaining her ideal weight.

## *More on Low Frustration Tolerance*

Almost always, achieving a long-term goal entails facing immediate discomfort. When we begin to pursue such a goal, we judge that the outcome is well worth the cost, but then somewhere along the line we get sidetracked. Since the cost is immediate and the benefit distant, it's easy to give in to the impulse to escape. Later, we regret deeply that we have failed to achieve the desired goal.

All this is perfectly natural and to be expected. If Tom keeps putting off studying for an important test in favor of watching movies, or if Sheila, who dreams of being a concert pianist, starts to skip practice to talk to friends on the phone, there is no need to introduce far-fetched "unconscious" explanations. To propose instead that Tom really dreads becoming a doctor because he identifies that profession with his father whom he hates without knowing it, or that Sheila unconsciously fears the plight of a concert superstar making millions from recordings, is fanciful in the extreme.

The universe simply isn't constructed in such a way that working toward an important objective is bound to be intrinsically delightful. The principle that applies in most arenas of life is the rule familiar to athletes and sports trainers: *No pain, no gain!*

## Schools Teach Addictive Thinking

Unfortunately, our culture reinforces the opposite, and potentially disastrous viewpoint. Fashionable discussion of education policy, for example, sometimes implies that learning ought to be sheer effortless enjoyment at every moment. Certainly, a skillful teacher will try to make the subject matter attractive and will know how to stimulate the students' interest, but nothing worthwhile can ever be *pure* fun—certainly not science, math, English, foreign languages, music, engineering, economics, history, or philosophy. Effective learning cannot be immediately pleasurable at *every* stage; success requires that students apply themselves and work hard, especially when it hurts.

The worst-hit victims of the "learning is fun" theory are often those from poor or disadvantaged backgrounds, because they are less likely to pick up at home the habits of discipline and application, which many middle-class students already bring to school with them.

Not only does the "learning is fun" fallacy tend to destroy scholastic achievement, it may reinforce Low Frustration Tolerance in every other area of life, and hence encourage addictions. School administrators who seek to remedy poor scholastic performance by making students feel good (instead of fostering self-discipline and rigorous academic standards) may indirectly be stimulating their students' interest in taking drugs.

By contrast, our children would benefit from being shown role models who forge ahead in boring, unexciting, uncomfortable conditions, to reach a valuable goal. It would be best to tell our children: "Life consists of one hassle after another, but you can cope, and you can derive deep satisfaction from overcoming those hassles. To accomplish anything worthwhile is going to be hard, tedious, and unpleasant at times, but you can do it. Only babies demand that every minute be free of discomfort or frustration; grown-ups tolerate frustration and realistically endure it as an inherent aspect of life."

## *Getting Burned Up About Frustrations*

Jon came to me just after he learned that his mother had lung cancer. He was 33, very upset about his mother, and even more worried about himself. Short, with distinguished-looking silver-grey hair and an attractive tan, he radiated businesslike self-confidence and in fact had an MBA and a CPA.

Beneath this dazzling exterior, Jon's stress, insomnia, and obsessive behavior were some of the issues that had initially brought him to therapy. He reported that he had difficulty relaxing, that he took his co-workers' opinions of himself too seriously, and that he felt guilty about missing deadlines at work. We had worked on these problems successfully using Three Minute Exercises, and had saved Jon's addiction to cigarette smoking for last.

Jon had started smoking when he joined a college fraternity. "Everyone else was smoking so it seemed like the thing to do." He had quit for five months in business school when he was dating a fellow student who objected to cigarettes. He later quit again for several months when he started with a firm of business analysts.

I asked Jon why he now smoked.

"I just can't stop. I've tried several times, and I've never been able to stay off for long."

"All that proves is that you haven't yet stopped smoking. It does not prove that you will not stop in the future."

"But surely the fact that I'm still smoking, after all my attempts to stop, proves that I can't stop."

"What it shows is that in the past you have found it very difficult to stop. But past failures don't prove future failure. Some of the great successes of history, like the invention of the electric light bulb, came after years of repeated failure."

## *Cooling the Turkey*

After persuading Jon that he might well stop smoking despite his past failures, I discussed the mechanics of quitting. The two most common strategies are cold turkey or tapering off. Most successful quitters have found the abrupt abandonment of the habit has worked, but gradually cutting back on the number of smokes a day seems more feasible to a substantial minority.

Jon preferred this more graduated approach. The first step is to keep an accurate running tally of all cigarettes smoked. Jon stashed a small pencil and piece of paper in his cigarette pack. Immediately *before* lighting up, he would mark the corresponding day on the paper. At the end of the week he could see at a glance how many he had smoked each day and for the whole week. We could then set up goals for the coming days and weeks, gradually tapering to zero.

During the first week of self-monitoring, Jon averaged two and a half packs a day, though by the end of the week he was down to a little over two packs. He achieved this by prohibiting himself from smoking during certain activities or in certain places. For example, he stopped smoking in his house, and stepped outside to have a cigarette. Jon also found that merely practicing self-monitoring led him to cut back, a common result of this practice.

### Jon's Three Minute Exercise

While he was tapering off, Jon did regular Three Minute Exercises on his Low Frustration Tolerance. Here is one:

A. (**A**ctivating event): I'm in my car, driving home from work. It was a rough day, and I'm stuck in traffic. I'm feeling stressed and I've a strong urge to unwind with a cigarette. Since I'm trying to cut down, I don't light up. Deprived of the cigarette, I'm now feeling even worse.

B. (irrational **B**eliefs): I MUST have a cigarette because I strongly want one. I CANNOT STAND the frustration of being so deprived. The discomfort is HORRIBLE.

C. (emotional **C**onsequences): Agitation.

D. (**D**isputing): Why MUST I have a cigarette, just because I strongly want one? Where is it carved in granite that I CANNOT STAND the frustration of being so deprived? What's the evidence the discomfort is HORRIBLE?

E. (**E**ffective thinking): No law of the universe says I MUST have a cigarette, even though I strongly want one. There is no evidence that the universe has singled me out as being entitled to a cigarette. I've always experienced frustration in my life. I always will, and no reason exists why I SHOULD not. I CAN STAND being deprived, although I don't like it. I am even capable of gaining considerable enjoyment from life with this deprivation. I'm determined to face the frustration and accept it. Life is hard, but I make it harder by bellyaching about it. Discomfort is just discomfort, not HORRORS. Life consists of one discomfort after another—tough! My greater problem is not the discomfort itself, but rather me horribilizing about it. Seen in the context of all human problems, my discomfort could easily be far worse. As I refrain from smoking, the discomfort will tend to diminish.

F. (new **F**eeling or behavior): Discomfort, rather than agitation.

## *Three Minute Imagery*

After Jon had written out a Three Minute Exercise, I instructed him in *Three Minute Imagery:*

**STEP ONE**

Vividly imagine, picture, or fantasize the following: You're in a situation where you feel tempted to smoke (relaxing after a meal, tense about a job interview, or bored with nothing to do). You're experiencing a distinct urge to smoke, but you resist.

**STEP TWO**

Now, as you vividly imagine this, allow yourself to feel anxious, depressed, or agitated about not lighting up. This is the same inappropriate emotion you normally feel whenever you find yourself in the situation in Step 1. Do Step 2 for only a few seconds.

**STEP THREE**

Still picturing the scene described in Step 1, make yourself feel concerned, disappointed, or appropriately frustrated—*instead of* anxious, depressed, or agitated. Since you create and control your own feelings, with persistence you can modify them. How can you make yourself feel concerned rather than anxious, disappointed rather than depressed, or appropriately frustrated rather than over-frustrated? Show yourself that you *can stand* frustration even though you don't *like* it; convince yourself that no law of the universe says you *must* have a cigarette merely because you strongly *want* one; remind yourself that discomfort and deprivation are just that and no more, never awful, terrible, or horrible.

Jon diligently practiced Three Minute Imagery for three minutes, twice a day. After six weeks he had completely weaned himself from his tobacco addiction. Two years later he reported that he was still cigarette-free. He had had one relapse, after eight months, but had quickly gotten back in control.

# 9

# *Panic Attacks: They Don't Come Out of the Blue*

*Reason can wrestle*
*And overthrow terror.*
> —EURIPIDES (484 B.C.–406 B.C.)

"I felt like I was about to die, or go crazy. I felt as if I was losing all control. It was blind panic—sheer terror!"

A shudder of remembered horror passed through the attractive, dark-haired woman seated opposite me. She was in control of herself, but was obviously under some strain. Even to speak of her unpleasant experience seemed like an ordeal. Her face was drawn and pale, her fingers pressed tightly against her purse as she related her experience.

"I was in a rush, and I got stuck in a slow-moving line at the supermarket," she told me, her voice quavering, almost on the verge of tears. "Out of the blue, I was gripped by feelings of terror, and I felt like I was suffocating. I had to get out of there. I left my grocery cart right in the line and ran out of the store.

"What a relief it was to get some air, but at the same time I really felt like an idiot for doing that. I felt ashamed of myself. I just went home, lay on the bed, and cried helplessly."

Kelly, a busy, efficient, 33-year-old executive, was, like millions of others, a sufferer from panic attacks.

## *What Panic Attacks Feel Like*

If you have never experienced a panic attack, then imagine how you might feel if you were trapped in a burning building, or if the plane you were on started diving and spinning out of control, or if you were captured by a maniac who told you he was going to gouge out your eyes. Under these alarming (and very unusual) circumstances, you might expect to feel panic or terror.

What happens in such situations is that your mind concludes that you are probably about to suffer intense physical pain followed by permanent injury or death. Your mind also evaluates this probable outcome as dreadful, terrible, or horrible. This split second mental evaluation causes various bodily events—your heart races, your bowels churn, your blood vessels expand causing an all-over hot sensation, and your mouth becomes dry. These physical symptoms are then labeled by the mind as "terror" or "panic."

The victim of panic attacks experiences these unpleasant sensations in normal, everyday situations *without* the disastrous or life-threatening provocation. There is no burning building, no out-of-control airplane, and no maniac bent on mutilation. Yet the terror surges up, apparently for no reason at all. With some victims, the terror obviously appears in specific situations; with other sufferers, it seems to come on at any time or place.

The fact that there is no obvious reason for these panic attacks is not usually a consolation to the sufferer. She feels all the more frightened since the panic is inexplicable to her, and therefore strange. Because of the inexplicability, there seems to be no way to predict or control the attacks, so there is usually the added fear that the attacks will get even worse, perhaps becoming "more than she can possibly stand."

144

# Panic Attacks: They Don't Come Out of the Blue

Kelly's frightening experience in the supermarket line was the latest in a series of similar episodes. It prompted her to consult a physician.

"He gave me all sorts of tests, but couldn't find a thing wrong with me. He said that physically I was in great shape, and that my trouble was all in my head. That's why he referred me to you. I feel as if I'm going crazy."

I asked Kelly how long she had been afflicted by these panic attacks. She told me they had been going on for two months. The first attack occurred when she was sitting on a bus.

"I was late for an important meeting. The bus was packed and stiflingly hot. All of a sudden, my heart started pounding, and I began feeling weak and light-headed. I started having crazy thoughts like: 'I'm losing my mind,' and 'I just have to get out of here right now or something dreadful will happen.'

"But I knew I dare not get off the bus because I would miss the meeting. After a few minutes of horrible anxiety, these feelings passed, and what a relief that was! But a week later they came back—again while I was on a bus—this time going to work. The anxiety and the crazy thoughts seemed to last twice as long as before. After that, every morning while getting ready for work, I would start worrying that these attacks would hit me again. To avoid them, I started taking a taxi to work, but I really don't want to keep on paying out for taxi fares. Anyway, the attacks have started hitting me in other situations, and they seem to be getting more and more frequent. I'm terrified that I'm going out of my mind."

People in Kelly's position often don't realize how very common such attacks of anxiety are. Millions of human beings suffer episodes of panic or intense anxiety, and millions more have suffered from them at some time in the past. The chances of these people going "out of their minds" (even in the broadest sense) are a lot less than the chances of any one of us being hurt in a serious traffic accident.

## The First Panic Attack Doesn't Begin with Panic

There is one important feature of panic attacks like Kelly's which we would do well to notice. The *first* incident does not *begin* with panic, intense anxiety, or terror. It usually begins with an unexpected physical discomfort, such as chest pressure or pains, rapid heartbeat, dizziness, weakness, shakiness, a mild case of the jitters, or feeling vaguely unsettled or weird. Frequently the sufferer later forgets or misremembers the first attack, and assumes that all the attacks have come "out of the blue," in the pure form of unalloyed terror. But, when asked to recall step-by-step exactly what happened in the first incident, she usually does remember that it started with physical discomfort or mild uneasiness.

But why do these physical symptoms occur in the first place? Often for no medically detectable reason—but neither are they a creation of deep, dark forces in the unconscious mind. Since we are all human, with imperfectly functioning physiologies, we are commonly vulnerable to such ephemeral physical symptoms. The anxiety-prone person, rather than ignoring these discomforts, dwells on them, thereby magnifying and prolonging them.

So I began by assuring Kelly that hers was a very common problem and one that I had treated frequently with success. I explained that first we would discuss how anxiety and panic work in general, and next we would apply this to her particular situation. I told Kelly that after a little discussion, she would possess the tools to start chipping away at her problem.

## *Panicky Feelings Come from "Musty" Thoughts*

Next, I explained a general psychological principle: "If you're anxious, or I'm anxious, or Sigmund Freud is anxious, it's never the objective situation alone that's making us feel that way, no matter how unpleasant that situation may be. Rather, it's our assessment or evaluation of the situation that's creating the emotion. Its our beliefs, our *thinking*, that determines our emotional response.

"For instance, suppose I'm about to deliver a speech to a large audience, and a few minutes before I begin I realize there's a possibility I might stutter during the talk. I might start thinking: 'I MUST not stutter. I MUST not stutter. I've GOT to give a good talk. I HAVE to impress these people. I SHOULD be invited back.' It's very likely that thinking this way, putting these demands on myself, I'll make myself anxious and greatly increase the probability that I will stutter.

"But now suppose it's the same situation; I'm going to give the talk to the same audience, and again I think of stuttering. But this time I view it differently. This time I *don't* think in terms of demands and absolutes. I think in terms of preferences. Then I will say to myself: 'I strongly PREFER not to stutter. I very much DESIRE to give a good talk. I keenly WISH to get invited back. I intensely HOPE to impress this audience.' Viewing it this way, it's probable I would not feel so nervous, and it's quite possible I would actually reduce my chances of stuttering."

Considering this scenario, apparently unrelated to her own problem, Kelly quickly agreed that my argument was quite reasonable.

I emphasized to Kelly that people create problems for themselves by turning their preferences into "musts"; however, the preferences themselves may be perfectly sensible. Preferences exist on a continuum from just barely

147

preferable to very, very highly preferable. You can acknowledge that some outcome is important to you and that you would very much like it to happen, without thereby concluding that it MUST happen. You can also accept that there may be something you would very much like that you are, as a matter of brute fact, unlikely to get.

## *Wishing for the Moon Is Harmless*

Some therapists think that the solution to their clients' problems is for the clients to abandon their "unrealistic" or "inappropriate" desires or wishes. But I believe that this usually doesn't get to the heart of the matter. A person may experience practical difficulties because her view of the world is inaccurate or unrealistic—for instance, if she invests a lot of time and energy in pursuing some goal that is in fact unattainable. I might do that person a favor by questioning the realism of her goal. But no *emotional* problem is caused by even the most fantastic desire or wish, as long as it is a preference and does not get turned into a "must."

## *Kelly's "Musts"*

Once Kelly had grasped the reasonableness of preferences as contrasted with demands and "musts," we applied this principle to her panic attacks. At first she sincerely denied having any thoughts at all preceding and during her panic attacks. So I recounted the most frequently occurring thoughts reported to me by other panic attack victims over the past twenty years. She immediately recognized some of them as her own.

These thoughts included:

- I MUST know precisely why I'm feeling like this

- I MUST be certain it's not serious

- I MUST never lose control or act crazily

- I MUST not do anything stupid or look foolish

- I MUST have a rock-solid guarantee I'm not about to do or go crazy.

- I MUST not make myself anxious I explained to Kelly that all these notions made perfect sense as preferences:

- I PREFER to know why I'm feeling like this

- I PREFER to be sure it's not serious

- I PREFER to never lose control or act crazily

- I PREFER not to do something stupid or look foolish

- I PREFER to know I'm not going to die or go crazy

- I PREFER not to make myself anxious

But by viewing these as "musts," Kelly increased her level of anxiety and her likelihood of experiencing anxiety and panicky feelings. The solution to the emotional problem consisted of Kelly's eliminating these very destructive demands she now realized that she was continually pounding into her head.

This solution involved two steps:

**STEP ONE**

The first step consisted of *recognizing* that the "musts"—but not the preferences—are entirely false and unfounded; that although it would be highly preferable to avoid great discomfort, it's never a "must"; that she doesn't always "have to" feel entirely comfortable, and she often won't; that although it might be wonderful for Kelly never to upset herself, she assuredly will do so occasionally, since she is an imperfect human being like the rest of us. In the worst–case scenario, Kelly might "lose control," go crazy, or even die. Similarly, she might be struck by lightning. This is unlikely, but if it does happen, it is very unfortunate and very sad. Although the worst-case scenario is highly improbable, it's unreasonable and unrealistic for Kelly to demand a cast-iron guarantee that it will not happen. No such guarantee is available to any human being.

**STEP TWO**

The second step consisted of Kelly thoroughly *convincing* herself of the truth of these insights. This would involve more than just nodding in agreement. It would mean confronting and disputing her "musts"—meaningfully, persistently, and vigorously—until she gave them up. Kelly was following my explanation intently because she began to see some hope for overcoming those dreaded feelings that had so frighteningly enveloped her for two long months. But she was a bit skeptical that the cure could be so simple. "Just repeat to myself 'I PREFER' instead of 'I MUST' and I won't get so upset?" she asked dubiously. "That's partly right. But if you really think it through rather than just mouthing the words, you'll get more mileage out of the process," I assured her. "Don't merely parrot these phrases, but go over them carefully many times until you really begin to believe and feel that they are true."

## *Practice Makes Progress*

Like many clients, Kelly had the idea in the back of her head that something could happen in therapy that would cause all her troubles to vanish, with very little effort on her part. I explained to Kelly that learning to think more rationally was a skill that required practice and sustained attention, just like learning any other skill.

Suppose that you want to play the piano but don't even know where middle C is. You listen to a few lectures about the piano or read a short book on the subject. You then practice for a couple of hours—and stop. It would be silly to expect to be able to play the piano. Everyone knows that it takes practice, practice, practice, every day for several years, to be able to reach a level of modest competence at playing the piano.

Changing your habitual thinking patterns isn't quite so difficult. You don't have to practice several hours a day for years on end. But at least a few minutes a day for a few months will probably be necessary. After all, you have spent most of your life so far inadvertently "practicing" thinking in terms of "musts." You won't change this overnight, just as you won't play a simple piece by Mozart after one week at the piano. But you will observe some small signs of progress almost immediately, and these will grow if you keep at it.

## *Kelly's Three Minute Exercise*

I explained to Kelly the Three Minute Exercises— simple-looking drills somewhat like the five-finger exercises, scales, and arpeggios employed by pianists. Since she seemed to agree with my arguments, or was at least convinced enough to give the method a try, we wrote out a

Three Minute Exercise for her to review every day in order to change her thinking:

A.  (**A**ctivating event): I'm sitting on the bus and for no apparent reason my heart starts racing, my legs get wobbly, and I feel light-headed.

B.  (irrational **B**elief): I MUST not feel this way.

C.  (emotional **C**onsequences): Anxiety, dread, panic.

D.  (**D**isputing the irrational belief): Why MUST I not feel this way?

E.  (**E**ffective new thinking): No eleventh commandment states that I MUST not feel this way. I strongly prefer not to feel so uncomfortable but discomfort won't kill me. I've survived it before and will survive it again. Although I distinctly do not like these symptoms, I can bear what I don't like. Humans commonly experience physical pain. I can accept that rather than eat myself up inside about it. This is a chance for me to face discomfort, not magnify it, and go on with my life. The more I am determined to confront it, rather than escape from it, the better off I'll be in the long run."

F.  (new **F**eeling): Concern rather than panic.

Within a few weeks, Kelly had greatly reduced her fear of panic attacks, and the attacks, when they came, passed quickly. Feeling now that she was able to make progress, she even began to look forward to the onset of symptoms as a golden opportunity to practice the technique, knowing that she could cope with the attack.

Within a couple more months, Kelly's ordeal was largely over. But that doesn't mean that she will never again suffer anxiety, or that she can now be guaranteed against ever having a panic attack.

We are all fallible human beings. We are all imperfect. None of us will ever achieve perfect rationality. In all probability, Kelly will occasionally experience episodes of anxiety at various times.

But having gone through two months of therapy and practiced her Three Minute Exercises consistently, Kelly was now far better equipped to nip anxiety in the bud. When anxiety appeared, she was able to invest three minutes to dispute her "musts" in writing. In this way, she successfully avoided the escalation of anxiety into panic attacks.

## Ashamed of Being Afraid

Panic attacks may occur at only one period in a person's life, or they may recur several times at intervals, or they may plague a person over a long period. These attacks are usually associated with fears of physical symptoms, fears of "losing control," fears of "going crazy," or of being trapped, being alone, or dying.

Another common theme is the dread of panicking which is felt to be a sign of personal weakness or inadequacy. The case of William, a 58-year-old high school principal, married with two grown children, is a good example.

William appeared hale-and-hearty, tall, handsome, and somewhat portly. He had an intense manner and seemed to take himself rather seriously. In explaining why he had come to see me, he related the following grim experience:

"Just about a month ago, on a hot summer day, I was in the County Office Building on an elevator that suddenly got stuck between floors. Since I have a history of atrial fibrillation, I got really scared about having a heart attack. Immediately, I felt my heart pounding uncontrollably.

"I panicked. I yelled 'Help! Get me out of here!' and banged on the elevator walls. After about thirty minutes, which seemed like a lifetime, an elevator repairman came and got me out through a trapdoor in the ceiling. I was drenched in my own sweat, and I felt like a fool.

"Now I panic just at the *thought* of taking an elevator. Living and working in a small town, I've found it fairly easy to avoid the few buildings with elevators. I can't use the stairs either, because I have chronically ailing knees, turning even a few flights of stairs into an ordeal.

"Six months ago my wife booked the two of us on a Caribbean cruise for our first real vacation in I don't know how many years. But last week she discovered that the liner has three levels and an elevator.

"Now I shudder at the thought of that elevator. I was looking forward to a wonderful vacation, but now it's a nightmare."

With some difficulty, William admitted to me that he was very ashamed of his fears. He was "petrified," he said, that his own fears would ruin the vacation, and he was already feeling ashamed that this might happen.

## Fear Is Nothing to Be Afraid Of

"A grown man behaving like a baby! I feel so humiliated. A mature person would just have waited quietly for the repairman. Now, I know that it's extremely unlikely that I'll ever again be stuck in an elevator. And even if I do get stuck, sooner or later someone would come and get me out, like last time. I know that the chances of my dying of a heart attack in a stuck elevator because medical aid can't reach me are about the same as being hit on the head by a meteorite.

"You don't need to tell me it's irrational. I tell myself that over and over again. I tell myself I'm being stupid and ridiculous, but this doesn't help. I'm still petrified at the mere thought.

"I have to do something about this. My wife insisted that I consult you. I doubt that you can do anything—it's just a last resort. I know I'm the only one who can help me, and I'm utterly defeated."

"You're not defeated at all," I said optimistically. "But you do have two very different emotional problems. First, you're making yourself panicky about getting trapped in the elevator and having a heart attack."

"You got that right," William affirmed sullenly. The tone of his voice said: "Tell me something I don't know."

"Second, you're making yourself *ashamed* about the prospect of getting a panic attack in the elevator."

"I'm *making* myself ashamed?"

"Correct. And what does making yourself ashamed accomplish?"

"I guess, just one more problem." William admitted reluctantly.

"Exactly right. Shame, further worry, and the greater likelihood that you'll *make* yourself panic in an elevator. You're mentally rehearsing for this great event. You're working yourself up to it."

"I know, I know. I tell myself it's ridiculous, but that doesn't help. In fact, the more I keep telling myself that the whole thing's plain silly, and I shouldn't get upset, the worse things seem to get."

"That's right," I told him. "Saying 'I SHOULD not panic' will make it worse. Since you haven't had any previous training in Three Minute Therapy, it's not really surprising that when you desperately try to help yourself you're likely to fail. Unfortunately, the public schools never taught you a few basic principles for maintaining your sanity. It's a rather simple message, and one that could help you immensely for the rest of your life."

William was now eager to hear that simple message. "Could I learn that now?" he asked.

"Certainly. Here's lesson one. Look for your 'must.' You have a 'must' such as 'I MUST not panic,' 'I MUST not act weakly,' 'I MUST not behave foolishly.' "

"That's right. That's what I keep telling myself. 'I MUST not panic.' "

"But that 'must' is responsible for your secondary problem. That 'must' consists of shame, anxiety, and panic and accounts for what blocks you from facing the elevators. But there's no evidence for the 'must,' is there?"

"I don't understand. You mean I *should* panic? I *should* make a fool of myself? But I don't want to panic."

"I agree. It's highly desirable not to panic or act foolishly. And we could list many good reasons why that's so. But listen more carefully to exactly what I'm saying. I'm not asking you, 'Why is it preferable not to panic or act weakly?' We agree it's not preferable. What I am asking is: 'Why MUST you not do what it's preferable not to do? You're an imperfect, fallible human being, like all human beings. Why aren't you allowed to make mistakes and act foolishly? What good reason could you possibly have for the unconditional demand that you never make mistakes or act foolishly? Isn't this about as reasonable as saying 'I MUST never catch a cold'?"

"Well," William said thoughtfully, "I don't know. Putting it that way, I guess I am allowed to make mistakes. I guess I am allowed to panic and act foolishly."

"Right. You're allowed to make mistakes. You're allowed to panic. You're allowed to function weakly. But what happens when you keep repeating to yourself: 'I MUST act my age. I SHOULD not panic or act foolishly. I MUST not be ridiculous or look ridiculous'? You're not allowing yourself to be imperfect. And that kind of thinking will almost always lead to shame, anxiety, panic—the exact opposite of what you would really like."

"I think I see what you mean."

William had reached the stage where he had some glimmering of the crucial insight that his preferences made sense, but as *demands* they were entirely unreasonable Once you have come this far, your task is to convince yourself of this truth, thoroughly and in detail. Although it may seem paradoxical, when you accept yourself—really accept yourself—as an imperfect individual subject to panic and other human failings, your feelings of anxiety are likely to diminish.

Rather than fearing fear, as FDR recommended, we can view the onset of fear as a golden opportunity to practice viewing fear rationally: as an extremely uncomfortable emotion rather than something horrible, awful, or terrible.

William wasn't immediately convinced. It took another session of discussion before he would accept that his 'musts' might lie at the root of his problem, and that a likely solution to his problem would be to work hard at combating these 'musts.' He could do this by disputing them *ad nauseum* and by deliberately creating and seizing opportunities to take elevators.

## *William's Three Minute Exercise*

So William was eventually persuaded to do the Three Minute Exercises on a regular basis. Here is an early example:

A. (**A**ctivating event): Suppose I get into an elevator, it gets stuck between floors, and I panic and act foolishly.

B. (irrational **B**elief): I MUST not panic or act foolishly.

C. (emotional **C**onsequences): Shame, anxiety, worse panic.

D. (**D**isputing the irrational belief): Why MUST I not panic or act foolishly?

E. (**E**ffective new thinking): Since I find panicking and acting foolishly extraordinarily unpleasant, I keenly prefer not to panic. But no good reason exists why I MUST never panic. After all, anxiety *is* part of the human condition. Being imperfect, I will act foolishly at times, but that merely demonstrates that I'm a fallible human like billions of other fallible humans—not a totally weak person. And given my vulnerable heart condition, it's understandable that I might get panicky, though I don't HAVE to. Facing the prospect of a panic attack is a definite disadvantage of going on the cruise, but in order to get the pleasures of the cruise, it's unavoidable to bear the displeasures associated with it. The more I face panic attacks and practice thinking rationally about them, the less I'll tend to upset myself in the long run, and that will minimize further attacks. The upcoming cruise is a fine opportunity to practice accepting panic and accepting my weaknesses, instead of magnifying them and running away from them.

F. (new **F**eeling): Great concern rather than shame about panic.

## *Bon Voyage!*

William practiced writing out his Three Minute Exercises at least once a day, causing this new way of thinking to become second nature to him. Then he was better able to tackle his initial fear of elevators. He accomplished this again using Three Minute Exercises, which he applied conscientiously.

On the morning of his embarkation for the cruise, he experienced only slight trepidation. On his return, William reported to me that he had taken the elevator a few times each day, at first with difficulty but then with only slight anxiety, and had thoroughly enjoyed the cruise. And he also assured me that whenever the thought of panicking crossed his mind he said to himself forcefully: "If I panic, I panic. Tough luck. I'll survive!"

# *10*

# *Money: You Make Your Own Misery*

*If you make money your god, it will plague you like the devil.*

—HENRY FIELDING (ca. A.D. 50–130)

"Last week in the city: It was pathetic. There was this woman, dressed in filthy rags, reeking to high heaven, a hopeless case, sitting on the sidewalk with her little boy. A cardboard sign round her neck said: 'HUNGRY', and she had an open box to throw coins in."

Eva, the 35-year-old middle-class lady who told me this grim recollection wasn't expressing the compassionate concern that we all feel. She was expressing the haunting fear that she might end up like the street person she had witnessed. She wanted to leave her husband, Brian, but was afraid of the financial consequences.

"Leaving Brian scares the daylights out of me. Me with my kids on the street. A total wreck. It haunts me whenever I think about escaping from him."

## *Possibilities Are Not Probabilities*

I asked Eva: "Why dwell on that gruesome scenario? You may just as well picture yourself diagnosed with cancer the next time you go for a checkup or being burned to a crisp in a flaming car crash the next time you drive to the supermarket. In fact, either of these is immensely more probable than that you would ever become homeless."

"Yes, I guess you're right. But when you mention those other grim scenarios, they're just like—unreal. The beggar woman picture is my nightmare. Unbelievably dreadful. Maybe something to do with my childhood. My parents had a bad attitude towards money. I guess I'll have to figure that out."

"Well, yes and no," I countered. "It would be helpful to figure out why your thoughts turn to this 'doomsday' scenario when you consider walking out on your husband. But the answer to that 'Why?' does not lie in your childhood, nor in your parents' attitudes. It lies in the way you think right now—in your demands, your 'musts' and your 'shoulds.'"

"Really?" Eva was clearly flabbergasted to hear this from a therapist. "I don't have to relive my childhood experiences? Wow, that's something to think about!"

## A Shattered Marriage

Statuesque, with long auburn hair, Eva had been married for ten years and had two young sons. Although still living with her husband, she was currently pursuing her third affair. Eva and Brian lived in a large, eleven-room house in a northern suburb of New York. She had a master's degree in fine-art photography and had constructed a dark room in the house's basement. Her excitable manner came across in a loose, tangential, free-associative way of talking.

Eva and Brian, a specialist physician, often argued about the kids, their in-laws, and money—especially Eva's excessive spending. Eva resented Brian and no longer felt any warmth toward him, but whenever she considered leaving, the specter of poverty would appear and paralyze her decision. Behind Eva's anxiety and indecision lay the demand: *I MUST have an iron-clad guarantee that if I leave Brian, life will not be financially difficult for me and the boys!*

I encouraged Eva to attack this poisonous notion by doing Three Minute Exercises. At first she balked at the self-discipline involved, but I assured her that after some practice it would amount to about three minutes a day. She soon became enthusiastic and started grinding out Three Minute Exercises at a furious rate. Here's one of many.

## Eva's Three Minute Exercise

A. (**A**ctivating event): Uncertainty about making it financially if I leave Brian.

B. (irrational **B**elief): I MUST have a guarantee that if I leave Brian I will succeed at making ends meet.

C. (emotional and behavioral **C**onsequences): Anxiety and indecisiveness.

D. (**D**isputing the irrational belief): Why MUST I have a guarantee that if I leave Brian I'll easily be able to make ends meet?

E. (**E**ffective new thinking): I don't NEED and can't reasonably EXPECT a guarantee that I'll make ends meet. I have no reason to suppose that God or the President will write me such a guarantee. There are no guarantees—except that we will all die someday, and even that isn't cast-iron, for we can't be sure that scientists won't devise a method to extend life indefinitely.

Demanding an unattainable guarantee practically guarantees that I'll make myself anxious,
and experience great indecision about leaving
Brian. I do have a reasonable probability that, if
I work conscientiously, I'll mostly have a steady
income, with occasional brief periods of unemployment.

F.  (new **F**eeling and behavior): No anxiety or indecisiveness, but concern and a serious endeav-
or to make the decision that's best for me.

Eva did finally move out, and later she unexpectedly started to date Brian. Their relationship improved now
that they were living apart and seeing each other less frequently. Eva dealt with the financial difficulties well. She
was glad she had made the break.

## *Sharona, The Sheepish Shoplifter*

A few weeks after Christmas, Sharona was sent to
me by the court. She had been apprehended in a local department store, stealing three expensive boys' shirts. "I
don't know what came over me," she said.

Sharona was a lean, dark-eyed woman, with eight
children. Her husband Emiliano worked in Chicago, and
stayed there Monday through Friday. He returned home, a
hundred miles south, on weekends. He worked as a security
guard, but his real talents lay in running up credit card bills
and parking tickets.

Although the family finances were shaky, Sharona
had not stolen the shirts out of sheer hardship. All the children had adequate clothes for school and for play. Sharona
soon disclosed to me that she had stolen several times before, without being caught, usually just before Christmas.

Her voice was filled with guilt and self-loathing, but also with genuine puzzlement at her dishonest behavior.

"I don't know why I did it," she told me tearfully. "I couldn't help myself."

I assured Sharona that we could quickly discover precisely why she had committed the crimes. We would simply pinpoint the thoughts in her head right before she reached for the shirts and stuffed them into her shopping bag.

"It was automatic. I wasn't thinking anything. I didn't know what I was doing. I saw the shirts and I reached out and took them," she whispered.

## The Motive Uncovered

I questioned her about the immediate background to the latest incident, and encouraged her to imagine, step by step, the detailed course of events in the clothing store.

"I was feeling bad that I couldn't get my kids some nice things for Christmas. We never seem to be able to make ends meet," she said. "Emiliano's always running up the credit card, buying things we don't need without consulting me. Like the other day he comes in carrying a new laptop computer—he'll probably never use it for anything except spaceship games." Her eyes opened wide. "I couldn't believe it. I never know what to tell the credit card companies when they call. They tell me I'm responsible for the payments too, even though he's the one spending." Tears welled up in her eyes.

"I think I hear a 'must' or a 'should' in there," I told her. "Can you see what it is?"

Sharona couldn't, so I explained that "compulsive" behavior—behavior you believe you have no control over—is generated by unrealistic or "musty" thinking. It probably begins with "Life must . . . ."

As Sharona's "musts" and "shoulds" surfaced, I reflected them back to her:

- Life MUST not consist of one financial hassle after another

- My situation MUST not be so unfair

- The Universe SHOULD supply me with an engraved warranty that my life will improve

- My kids MUST not be deprived of all the little extras that my friends' kids nearly all have

- My kids MUST not feel bad

- I SHOULD provide my kids with more

- My fairy godmother SHOULD protect me from the consequences of my stealing

- It SHOULD not be so difficult to make ends meet

After a little coaching, Sharona was able to see the connection between her "musts" and her "out of control" actions. She felt particularly overwhelmed by "Life MUST not consist of one financial hassle after another" and worked conscientiously on that. Here's one of her Three Minute Exercises:

## Sharona's Three Minute Exercise

A. (**A**ctivating event): The bill collector phoned. Three overdue parking tickets arrived in the mail. Emiliano bought a speedboat on credit.

Christmas is coming, and there's no money left to buy the children decent presents.

B. (irrational **B**elief): Life MUST not consist of one financial hassle after another for a poor slob like me.

C. (emotional and behavioral **C**onsequences): Self-pity, crying, compulsive stealing.

D. (**D**isputing the irrational belief): Why MUST life not consist of one financial hassle after another? How does having financial hassles magically turn me into a poor slob?

E. (**E**ffective new thinking): Reality is reality, not what I think it MUST be. It's a shame that I have great financial problems, but hardly the end of my life. No one has decreed that I run the Universe, so nothing says that my life MUST not involve money worries. Life has always consisted of one frustration after another, it always has and it always will. No reason exists why it SHOULD not. At worst, I'll have serious financial hassles for the rest of my life—but they're just hassles, obnoxious pains in the rear end, not horrors, terrors, or catastrophes.

There's no evidence that I'm a weak slob with no control over my fate. I'm imperfect and I make mistakes. Like every other human who ever existed, I act weakly at times, but that hardly qualifies me as a worthless, weak person.

F. (new **F**eeling and behavior): Discomfort and dissatisfaction, but no self-pity or stealing.

Within a few weeks, Sharona's thinking was strikingly more realistic. When I heard from her last, she was long off probation and had not stolen for the past three Christmases. She had not succeeded in reforming her spendthrift husband, and had decided that, given all her circumstances, it was better to tolerate him than to shoot him or walk out. As far as I know, she is realistically putting up with her constrained financial position, rather than ripping herself up inside about her husband's behavior.

## Money Management for the Clueless

Money worries afflict people at all income levels. I have had clients with six-figure salaries who have made themselves sick with anxiety about their finances. I've also known many people getting less than half of the national average salary who have been free of financial anxiety. People who do suffer from money worries imagine that at some higher level of income—usually about twice their current income—their financial fears would vanish. This belief is nearly always mistaken because money worries aren't caused by the objective financial circumstances. They are caused by a person's foolish thinking.

There are many books and other sources of advice on financial management. This book does not compete with them. However, some people easily intimidate themselves about even the simplest books and lectures from the experts because they get a glimpse of a world that seems as complex as quantum physics. A few guidelines could help immensely.

It's not true that "If a thing's worth doing at all, it's worth doing well." Some things are only worth doing poorly, and some things are much better done poorly than not done at all. If you don't know the difference between a

NOW account and an IRA, it's worth learning some simple principles which will help you. (However, you may want to pursue this a bit further. The effort and time needed to absorb a simple guide to personal finances, available on the Internet, is about the same as that required to follow a TV soap for a few weeks and probably slightly more entertaining.)

Whatever your circumstances, bear in mind two principles:

1. Unless someone just happens to give you a substantial sum, enough to live comfortably without working, there's only one *reliable* way to improve your financial position: work, save, and invest your savings.

2. Low-risk investments have low rates of return. Investments with high rates of return are risky—the higher the return, the greater the risk. Any proposition that seems to contravene this rule is sure to be a scam.

## From Rags to Riches

Let's consider the circumstances you might be in: If you're down and out, sleeping in the streets and in a Salvation Army center, the way to financial improvement is to get a regular job. (You don't *have* to do this; there's no "must" about it, but it's what's required if you aim to have a good chance of being significantly better off a couple of years down the road.)

Probably any job you're likely to get will be tedious, harsh, and low-paying. This increases the temptation to going back to being a street person, but if you put up with the job for six months, it may not seem so onerous, and you'll be more likely to find a better job.

It will be to your advantage to work hard, show up on time, every time, and be invariably polite and obliging, regardless of provocations.

Now let's suppose that you have a steady job with a well below-average income. It's a useful idea to start saving—even a small amount per pay period. You can put the money in a savings account. Your initial goal is to save enough so that you can live for six months without working. This will mean that, if you lose your job, you'll be able to take some time looking for a better job.

The next step is to increase your earnings. You may find it useful to take evening courses at your local community college to gain marketable skills. Get into the habit of scanning the "Help Wanted" sites to become familiar with what jobs are available and what the qualifications are. But ignore all claims that you can make fantastic sums with little effort. No matter what anyone tells you, there are *always* hundreds of job openings in any city. You could also look for jobs that have promotion prospects. Remember that in low-to-average paying jobs, it's steady reliability that most impresses supervisors. For example, there are always jobs available to people with a clean driver's license, a little driving experience, and a smidgen of presentability. You can make it a goal to acquire these three attributes.

Now we'll suppose you have made it into a close-to-average income position. You can either live strictly within your means, or you can accumulate debt. Both alternatives have their advantages and disadvantages. (The advantage of the latter is that you more quickly enjoy the things you buy. This may be particularly advantageous if you are buying durable equipment that will provide services for many years, like a personal computer.)

Most people find it best to take up a position somewhere between these extremes. It's generally unwise to rely on credit for regular consumer spending, like meals, unless you pay off the debt with the very next bill—credit card rates are very high. You can easily find yourself hovering around your credit limit and paying the interest on that amount with little lasting benefit to you.

Every time your income rises, increase your savings, even if only slightly. Keep a check on where your money goes. If I ask you right now: "What percentage of your take-home pay do you spend on food/accommodation/clothing/reading material/drinks and smokes/going out and having a good time?" can you immediately give a fairly accurate response?

Once you have a good handle on your expenses, you can think more seriously about how to reduce them. Do you buy any magazines you don't read all the way through? Could you skim them by visiting the local library? Could you cut down your eating bills? If you find it difficult to find ways to cut, try this exercise: Once you know where your money goes, imagine that your income is abruptly cut by ten or twenty percent and there is nothing you can immediately do to restore your present income. You would then *have* to cut your spending by a similar amount. What would you cut? Write it down and look at it. Now, carefully consider: Would you rather have what you're currently spending that money on, or would you rather have a growing nest egg that may prove extremely useful for the rest of your life?

The sheer power of steady, accumulated saving is often underestimated. If you save $1,000 per year at an interest rate of 10 percent and keep saving all the interest, you will have $63,000 after 20 years, and $181,000 after 30 years. But remember, you have no duty or obligation to save. It's simply a wise thing to do if you aim to improve your financial position.

## *Danielle's Dilemma*

In response to my opening query: "How can I be of help to you?" most clients immediately relate their short-comings, failures, interpersonal conflicts, and a whole host of other woes. Danielle was different. This petite 39-year-old, with an open, oval face and scarlet fingernails, began in an upbeat tone:

"I love people. I'm honest and sensitive. Being health-conscious is important to me." But Danielle wasn't free of troubles. She had split up with her boyfriend and was experiencing deep depression and guilt about supposedly having failed to make the relationship work.

Surprisingly, Danielle began the third session with an as yet undisclosed issue concerning both her work situation and her rapidly deteriorating finances. Her employment history consisted of a string of offbeat and varied occupations, including landscaper, freelance men's personal fashion advisor, and bartender. Currently, she was a customer representative for a major credit card company.

Danielle was in mounting debt. She was paying off loans on a car and other major purchases. She frequently got "disconnect" bills from the phone company and warning letters from her landlord about late rent. Much of her depression related to her financial straits.

As soon as I began to explain the concept of "shoulds" and "musts," Danielle rattled off a bunch of her own "musts," as if they were well-rehearsed—which, of course, they were!

"Life MUST not be so unfair as to give me such financial hassles! Life MUST give me everything I want, including a flashy car, unlimited credit, gourmet dining, modern furniture, and exotic travel! I MUST keep up with the Joneses! I MUST have a good credit rating—and there's something rotten about me if I don't! I MUST not disappoint the bill collectors! I MUST not get evicted and end up on the street! I MUST not seem poor to others, and I'm worthless if I do!"

## *From Misconceptions to New Directions*

I discussed with Danielle her major "musts" and their antidotes:

*Life MUST not be so unfair as to give me such financial hassles!* "It sometimes helps to consider the worst-case scenario and learn to accept that," I told Danielle. "Let's assume the worst, that life is utterly unfair to you. Can you think of any reason why it shouldn't be?"

Danielle couldn't think of any reason.

"The Universe is hardly under any obligation to treat you fairly," I continued. "And is it really true that life is unfair to you? You don't have a painful, terminal illness. You weren't born into a starving family in Ethiopia. In fact, your standard of living is far higher than that of the vast majority of humans who have ever lived or are alive today. What have you ever done to deserve such favored treatment?" She was amused to see her situation in that light.

*Life MUST give me everything I want, including a flashy car, unlimited credit, gourmet dining, modern furniture, and exotic travel!* "The technical term for that kind of thinking is 'Low Frustration Tolerance,' " I informed her, in a half-joking manner. "It's a fact that life consists of one deprivation, one inconvenience, one hassle, after another. If you demand that you alone be exempt from frustration, this implies that you *should* be magically protected from the normal stresses of living."

"But can't I dream about having all these things?" she asked plaintively.

"Certainly you may dream. There's nothing wrong with dreaming, as long as you know that it is indeed dreaming. You can even do better than dreaming. Once you give up the angry demand that you be free from life's slings and arrows, you will find it easier to methodically pursue some or all of what you dream about. You will then be more likely to turn at least some part of your dream into reality."

"That sounds good," she smiled.

"But let's be realistic," I said. "If you achieved every one of these things—and you probably could if you disciplined yourself to be clear-headed and hard-working enough—you would no doubt find daily life somewhat easier, but life would not be continuous, unremitting bliss. You can be sure that you would develop new wants, new unrequited preferences, and you would experience new frustrations." After a couple of minutes pondering and discussing this, Danielle wholeheartedly agreed.

*I MUST keep up with the Joneses!* Many therapists try to get their clients to abandon such a "futile" and "superficial" goal as keeping up with the Joneses. On the contrary, I view such a goal as legitimate and reasonable. But like all human goals, no Law of the Universe states that it *must* be achieved.

I pointed out to Danielle that she had other goals, as well as keeping up with the Joneses. She could successfully pursue some of these other goals, even if the Joneses continued to outstrip her.

I also emphasized the point that the mere objective fact that she earned less than the Joneses had no power to make her miserable. Only her own view of the situation, her own emotional judgment on the facts, could make her

174

feel wretched. She could compare her income and wealth with those of the Joneses, and be motivated to acquire more than they, without making it a "must" or rating her *self* in terms of the outcome.

The message soon began to sink in. "If I have less than the Joneses, so be it," she concluded. "I guess I'd better stop bellyaching about it."

*I MUST have a good credit rating—and there's something rotten about me if I don't!* "A poor credit rating does not rate YOU, *in toto.* It's just a statement about one of the millions of aspects of you. You have good traits, bad traits, and neutral traits—and you have the potential to improve many of your bad traits. The bad traits show that you are an imperfect person; they don't show that you're a *bad* person.

"Also, credit ratings are not entirely static. They change, and you have some control over that. Simply by making payments promptly from now on, you can ensure that your credit rating will eventually improve."

In trying to tackle Danielle's guilt about her poor credit rating, I emphasized that having a flaw doesn't make anyone worthless. "Every human walking the face of the Earth has major flaws," I contended.

*"Major* flaws? Oh, I can think of a few people who really seem to have it together," she said skeptically.

"You often won't realize it unless you know them intimately," I pointed out. "And even then they could keep their deficits hidden by limiting their lives. For example, someone with a fear of flying may avoid air travel, or someone who feels quite insecure under pressure will lose herself in a fairly safe, predictable job that doesn't challenge her abilities to the full. People often arrange their lives so that their flaws are inconspicuous, but the flaws are there!"

*I MUST not disappoint the bill collectors!* The core of this "must" is excessive concern with disapproval. It's not necessary to avoid other people's disapproval, especially people like bill collectors with whom you will have no contact in your daily life.

Of course it would be good to have no debts and be free from bothersome calls by bill collectors. But Danielle seemed more concerned with protecting the bill collectors from disappointment than with protecting herself from their nuisance. "I can't think of any practical disadvantages of their not liking me," admitted Danielle thoughtfully.

"So you're just worried about the wheels turning in their heads. If the bill collectors hate you, they hate you. How unfortunate! They have been disappointed before and they'll be disappointed again. Actually, they probably think very little about you personally—you're just one more case to them. Since people like you keep them employed, they have every reason to feel grateful to you. But even if they do hate and despise you, that's their problem!"

*I MUST not get evicted and end up on the street!* "That certainly would be unpleasant and sad, but hardly the end of the Universe," I argued. "And how likely is it that you would end up on the street?" I asked, trying to inject some reality.

"Well, if it came to it, I guess I could stay with a friend, or my aunt, until I got back on my feet," she mused.

"Right. Like the vast majority of people, you're more likely to be struck by lightning several times in one week than to end up on the street. And if you did somehow 'end up' on the street, you'd be off it again, with a job and an apartment, within a week or two. But still, suppose you did end up on the street. That's unpleasant, but you can stand unpleasantness, even extreme unpleasantness, although you don't like it."

## Money: You Make Your Own Misery

*I MUST not seem poor to others—and I'm worthless if I do!* "Most people you meet really won't care if you're poor," I told Danielle. "A few may dislike you for being poor. Some will actually like you for being poor. This is a statement about other people's likes and dislikes, not about your worth as a person."

"Their opinions of you exist only inside their brains. Science fiction movies to the contrary, their brains cannot emit fearsome death rays which make your stomach churn, raise your blood pressure, or muddle your thinking. But your brain—and only *your* brain—can indeed emit such 'rays' though they are really hormonal and electrical messages rather than rays. This isn't science fiction, but medical fact."

After a few sessions, Danielle calmed herself down about her financial status. Now able to view her situation more objectively, she decided to stay with her present position in order to build up seniority and become eligible for scheduled raises and promotions, and she made various adjustments in the way she did her personal bookkeeping. Currently, in therapy, she is working on her loneliness about not being in a relationship and her low frustration tolerance about taking the initiative to find the kind of man she hopes to marry.

# 11

## Compulsive Drinking: Don't Swallow the AA Brew

*Whether life is worth living may depend upon the liver.*
—ANONYMOUS

Alcoholics Anonymous (AA) is a highly active multimillion dollar organization, whose name is very familiar to most people. It has fathered numerous other self-help groups run on similar principles, like Gamblers Anonymous, Overeaters Anonymous, and Smokers Anonymous.

Some readers may be amazed that I would even think of criticizing AA. Isn't it just a mutual support group for people trying to stop drinking? And doesn't it actually enable a lot of people to stop drinking? Who could object to that?

In fact AA is a religious organization with some very specific views, deriving from the religious body known as "The Oxford Group Movement" or "Moral Rearmament," associated with Frank Buchman, who was extremely controversial both because of his political views (he said some friendly things about Hitler) and because of his intrusive, hard-sell methods of proselytizing.

AA is now quite independent, it is far from being a narrow sect, and most AA members have never heard of Buchman. Indeed, Buchmanism as a distinct sect has largely passed away. But AA was founded by two members of Buchman's movement, and most AA members share ad-

herence to the famous "12 Steps." The 12 Steps, or principles, are the philosophy behind the AA approach. As a matter of historical fact, the 12 Steps did derive from Buchman's teaching (see the recommended reading at the end of
this book). Many AA members still regard the 12 Steps
with reverential awe, as an absolute creed almost equivalent to the Ten Commandments. Incidentally, a court has
found that AA is a religious organization, and that therefore
requiring alcoholic offenders to go to AA, by favoring one
religious sect, is an unconstitutional breach of the separation of church and state.

AA has been so successful at disseminating its distinctive views that many people suppose that these views
are not controversial. For example, AA holds that "once
you're an alcoholic, you're always an alcoholic." According to AA there can be no such thing as an ex-alcoholic or
former alcoholic. Hence the well-known statement ritually
made at AA meetings: "I am an alcoholic." It is never, "I
*was* an alcoholic"—even if the individual has not taken a
drink for years.

Associated with this belief is the notion that alcoholism is a *disease* for which there is no cure, and that the
only salvation for the alcoholic is to give up drinking alcohol *completely and at once*. People influenced by AA propaganda are usually quite surprised to discover that many re-
searchers who have studied problem drinking do not agree
with any of this. Excessive drinking is not a bodily ailment,
something over which the individual has no control, and
many people who have had serious problems of overdrinking have been able to reform their habits so that they
can then engage in moderate, enjoyable, and harmless
drinking. (Some research indicates that moderate intake of
alcohol with meals is beneficial and leads to a longer life.)
Some problem drinkers find it easier to curtail an addiction
by gradual tapering off than by abrupt "cold turkey." More

often, the best strategy for overcoming compulsive drinking involves total abstinence for many years or even for a lifetime.

## *Brad's Bender*

Bradford, a likable, blond 23-year-old, came from a wealthy Texas family but had left home at 18 to hitchhike across the U.S. with the vague notion that he would "seek his fortune." When his money ran out in Portland, he decided to stay there. After two years of bumming around he started to experiment with drugs, including heroin and crack cocaine. His strained relations with his family became worse, and the family's financial and emotional support was reduced to a thin trickle. He felt spurned by them and became a heavy drinker, working only sporadically and living in a rundown apartment in a squalid neighborhood.

Dissatisfied with his life and looking for help, Bradford contacted AA, attended AA meetings regularly, and stopped drinking. After a few months on the wagon, he went on a bender and then began to drink so heavily that gainful employment was out of the question. Brad's family gave him an ultimatum: "Get into therapy, and we'll pay for it, or you will never see another penny from us as long as you live." And that's how Brad came to me.

As I questioned Brad closely about his drinking, it became clear that he had thirstily imbibed the AA message. When he had one drink after months of abstinence, he was totally convinced of the AA dogma that having a second and a third drink was not *an option* but *an automatic response*. A voice in the back of his head reminded him of what he had learned in AA meetings: "Remember, Brad, you are powerless over the bottle! You have no choice; it's a symptom of your illness."

Brad still believed this, of course, when he came to see me, and he had been inclined to believe something like it even before he had joined AA. Many movies, novels, and songs tell us that unfortunate or disliked behavior is not under the individual's rational control. AA was a finishing school for Brad who now firmly believed: "I'm an alcoholic for life!" Brad's case was therefore a long, hard, uphill struggle, since he had to be dissuaded of intellectual convictions that he had held most of his life and that were endlessly reinforced by popular culture.

One of Brad's sticking points was his opinion that heavy drinkers never stop of their own accord. I was able to prove him wrong by citing such cases as Robert Redford, Bing Crosby, Mickey Mantle, Frank Sinatra, and Johnny Carson, all of whom ceased their heavy drinking without any help from AA or professional counselors (See *The Truth about Addiction and Recovery* by Peele, Brodsky, and Arnold).

It took Brad several debates with me and many Three Minute Exercises to completely disabuse himself of the wrong beliefs that were plaguing him. (He also came to understand that other people, including his family members, did not HAVE to like him, respect him, or help him.) He eventually got his drinking completely under control, and the last time I had contact with him he had passed six years as a moderate, social, and occasional drinker. He had worked steadily, with several promotions, in a new career at a health club, had restored cordial relations with his family, and was happily married. Brad knows that a person who drinks heavily, with sadly unfortunate consequences, is currently choosing to behave foolishly, but is not sick or possessed, and does not need a doctor or an exorcist.

Here is one of the best of the Three Minute Exercises Brad employed to disinfect his "musty" thinking:

A. (**A**ctivating event): I went on a drunken binge after staying sober for five weeks.

B. (irrational **B**eliefs): I MUST never have a single relapse from sobriety. Since I have had a relapse, this proves I'm powerless over my drinking problem.

C. (behavioral **C**onsequence): Continued drinking.

D. (**D**isputing): Why MUST I not have a single relapse? Where's the evidence that having a relapse proves I'm powerless over my drinking?

E. (**E**ffective new thinking): No law of the universe (AA notwithstanding) says I MUST never have a relapse or I'm an incurable "alcoholic." Relapses and setbacks are part of any learning process—two steps forward and one step back! But if I'm convinced that I'm a powerless victim of my addiction, then my silly beliefs may cause me to turn normal setbacks into a life of alcoholism.

   I control my decisions and actions. If I pick up a glass and pour the contents down my throat, that is my action, and obviously I am in control of it. I can choose to cut down my drinking to a sensible level, and if this is important enough to me, I can plan, scheme, plot, and conspire to achieve that end. This won't be easy— why SHOULD it be? There may be further relapses, but there is simply no evidence that I'm fated to fail.

F. (new **F**eeling): Determination to make sensible decisions about drinking, but no superstitious dread of a single drink.

## *Twelve Steps to Chronic Dependence*

AA's First Step states: "We admitted we were powerless over alcohol, that our lives had become unmanageable." This is a fundamental tenet of the AA religion. The individual is powerless over the Demon Drink and must acknowledge it. Only with the help of a "higher power" can any individual control his or her drinking problem. No less than six of the 12 Steps refer directly to the supernatural power AA calls "God."

The AA recruit is told that without the help of a supernatural power, he has no choice but to continue to imbibe recklessly. This claim is false. Many people recover from habitual drunkenness on their own. But someone convinced of this false dogma has a ready excuse for giving up the struggle for self-control: "I didn't attack that bottle of Johnnie Walker: it attacked me!"

The dogma of individual powerlessness leads the individual to seek to serve the "higher power," which in practice means the group of people who represent that higher power. The individual exchanges dependency on the bottle for dependency on a lifetime's supply of AA meetings. While this is easier on the liver, it undermines personal independence and clear thinking.

The dogma of powerlessness is allied with the AA theory that drunkenness is an incurable disease, and that therefore everything hangs upon not taking that first drink. Swallowing a single drink is regarded as a catastrophe. AA converts are taught that if they succumb to temptation just once, they will automatically relapse into all the berserk behavior of the benighted boozer.

This wrong-headed and scientifically questionable theory encourages extremist thinking: "At all costs, I MUST not take a single drink." It means that when the individual has one drink, he may believe that his struggle for

184

sobriety is already lost, so he might as well give up and go on an alcoholic binge.

Paradoxically, the "one drink and you're lost" theory may also be harmful in just the opposite way. The individual has a single drink, discovers he is still in control of his behavior, and begins to feel blithely overconfident about the dangers of drinking. It would be better if a person with a past history of excessive drinking thought: "That drink I have just consumed sounds a warning bell. If I have a few more drinks right away I will be taking a serious risk."

A similar danger lies in the U.S. government's propaganda in its "war on drugs." Much of what the government says about drugs is so exaggerated and melodramatic that those people who are frequently around drug users *know* that the government's claims are hopelessly overblown and inaccurate. This may lead such people—the very people most at risk to serious drug abuse—to pooh-pooh the real dangers. There is, for example, no substance which automatically leads to dependency after one dose, or even several, and to talk as though there is such a substance encourages many young people with direct experience of drugs to discount all warnings about their harmful effects.

## *Am I an Alcoholic?*

Andy looked a bit like the stereotypical gangster out of a grade B movie: black hair slicked back, pencil-thin mustache, toothpick dangling from his lower lip, dark gray double-breasted pinstripe suit, and glossy black Oxford shoes. In partnership with his father, he owned and managed a successful clothing manufacturing plant. He led an exciting life, traveling to exotic corners of the world, sometimes in his own plane or yacht. Andy had a lavishly well-appointed home and a beautiful wife with expensive tastes, which he could well afford to indulge and thoroughly enjoyed indulging. He also had a serious drinking problem.

"Am I an alcoholic?" was Andy's main concern when he came to see me. He had imbibed enough AA propaganda to be convinced of the view that the world is divided into alcoholics and nonalcoholics, and that the application of this label explains everything.

I informed Andy that I do not regard it as helpful to view people as "alcoholics." I see them rather as individuals in their own right, possessing innumerable traits—good, bad, and neutral. People make mistakes, but it can be misleading to turn the mistakes into nouns and speak as though the mistake is the person.

"All right. So I'm not an alcoholic. But I guess I do drink too much, and I can't seem to keep my drinking under control. I'm not miserable, and I really get a kick out of life. So why do I drink so much?"

Andy couldn't understand why he was turning increasingly to alcohol when life had so much to offer him. He feared that he might be afflicted by a genetic defect that made him prone to alcohol dependence (one of his grandfathers had had the reputation of a notorious drunk).

Questioning Andy, I noticed a pattern: He had begun his drinking socially and moderately, then had gradually become aware that he could deal with the slightest anxiety by drinking, even when alone.

"You may be using alcohol to run away from something," I suggested.

"But what could I be running away from?" he queried.

"The one distinctly unpleasant, uncomfortable emotion you experience in your life—anxiety."

"I don't think that's it," he responded. "I'm hardly ever anxious."

"Exactly. But that could be part of the pattern I have in mind. Is there something you nearly always do whenever you *anticipate* feeling anxious?"

"Well, I dunno, have a drink, I suppose. Oh, I see. Maybe you do have a point there."

"I think so. And what is it that you tell yourself just before you take a drink?"

"That I am about to feel upset or apprehensive—and that I don't need that. So I'll have a couple of drinks and feel better."

"Yes, you're concerned that you might feel anxious."

"And that's why I drink?"

"Not exactly. It's not the anticipation of the anxiety that makes you drink. It's what you're telling yourself about that anxiety."

"What I'm telling myself . . . ?"

"Right. How you view the prospect of feeling anxious. What it means to you."

"Oh, that I don't like it."

"More than that."

"That it's AWFUL. That I CAN'T STAND it?"

"Exactly!"

"Do I really tell myself that?"

"Yes. Your basic philosophy is that you MUST feel relaxed and comfortable, and it's TERRIBLE if you don't, even for a few minutes. So when the specter of anxiety rears its head, your instant, panicky reaction is that this is not to be tolerated for a moment, especially when there is an easy, comfortable, short-term escape."

Andy was not berating himself for having emotional problems. He was not worried about *himself*, but he was worried about *discomfort*. To make progress, Andy trained himself to embrace the fact that anxiety and discomfort, though unpleasant, can be survived and accepted.

## *Andy's Three Minute Exercise*

A. (**A**ctivating event): In a few hours I have a business meeting with my father in which I will let him know that I was late in placing an order, so that certain fabrics were not delivered when we needed them. I anticipate that when he hears this he will go through the roof. I'm getting anxious about this.

B. (irrational **B**elief): Life MUST be free of anxiety. I CAN'T STAND being anxious. I MUST escape with a gin.

C. (behavioral **C**onsequence): Swallow six gins.

D. (**D**isputing): What's the evidence life MUST be anxiety-free? What's the evidence I can't stand being anxious?

E. (**E**ffective new thinking): I don't like this temporary anxiety, but I can stand it. I am perfectly capable of tolerating what I intensely dislike, including extreme discomfort. Although a few gins would make me feel better for the moment, it's destructive in the long run, so I will refuse to give in to the temptation for immediate escape. Impulsively escaping anxiety through drink just sets me up for lifelong problems. I'm determined to accept discomfort as an unavoidable aspect of being human.

F. (new **F**eeling): Acceptance of some discomfort as part of life and willingness to tolerate some anxiety rather than drinking to flee from it.

With exercises like these, Andy's interest in drinking waned. In turn, he became a more responsible business partner, so that he and his father began to get along better. These changes in Andy's life did not come quickly or easily, but rather as the result of concentrated, regular, and sometimes tedious practice, repetition, and reinforcement.

## *Staying Sober*

"I'm the world's leading expert on quitting drinking," Lonny told me, making a joke I've heard countless times about all forms of addiction. "I've done it so many times."

A close look at Lonny's otherwise handsome, intelligent face revealed the beginnings of the blotchy redness caused by broken capillaries, indicative of heavy drinking. Lonny was 53 years of age, had been not too happily married for 35 years, and told me he had been drinking heavily "off and on" for nearly 30 years.

Lonny had a relapse problem. He had many times decided to stop drinking alcohol, but in every case he had "slipped" and gone back to heavy drinking. I introduced Lonny to *Three Minute Refutations*, a technique for defeating the tendency to relapse.

Three Minute Refutations are a matter of recognizing the thoughts—the excuses—that encourage drinking and then demolishing these excuses. Here are some of the common excuses:

- This will be the last time I drink

- I've done so well lately, I can have one little drink

- It's been a hard day, I'll just have one to unwind

- Everyone else is drinking at this party, so how can it hurt if I join them?

- I'll just finish the wine in the cupboard before I stop altogether

- If I don't have a drink now, I won't get to sleep, and then I'll be a wreck tomorrow

## *Lonny's Search and Destroy Mission*

Three Minute Refutations involve the "search and destroy" mission: First recognize the addictive excuses, then get rid of them by answering them with defensive missiles—the refutations. One way to do this is to write out the excuses and then write out the refutations.

Here's one that we came up with in Lonny's case:

### *Excuse:*

"It's OK to drink right now, because it'll be the last time."

### *Refutations:*

1. Previous "last times" never were. What makes me think this would be different?

2. This "last time" could mean losing my job and ruining my career.

3. How many days is this bender going to last?

4. When I say to myself, "this is the last time," I know I'm lying.

5. If I can make this next time "the last time," why can't I make the last time "the last time?"

6. If I refuse to imbibe now, the discomfort will be temporary, not forever.

7. This "last time" could destroy my marriage.

8. This is just an excuse to drink—pure and simple.

Whenever you feel the urge to drink, identify the thoughts that make drinking seem reasonable. Then you can launch the counterattack.

When practicing Three Minute Refutations, it's often not enough to say the sentences over to yourself. It's usually far better to write them out. And it's even better, having written them out, to read them, preferably out loud, no less than five times a day. The object is to train yourself, so that when an excuse appears, you instantly recognize it, and instantly respond with a barrage of smart missiles: the refutations.

## The Sober Truth About Problem Drinking

The root cause of alcoholism is unrealistic thinking. Such thinking can be changed, and in this way addictive behavior can be overcome.

Alcoholics Anonymous has some good points—for instance, emphasizing the present rather than the past. It helps some people terminate their alcohol addiction, but AA teachings make it more difficult for other people with drinking problems to change their ways. AA encourages replacing addiction to alcohol with addiction to a religious movement.

Finally, here are some of the ways in which Three Minute Therapy differs from AA:

1. Three Minute Therapy is derived from a scientifically developed, coherent theory of psychotherapy, Rational Emotive Behavior Therapy, whereas AA is an essentially religious organization, its teachings adapted from the Oxford Group Movement.

2. The theory underlying Three Minute Therapy has been supported by hundreds of rigorous studies published in the psychological literature, whereas AA's claims about the nature of alcoholism and its treatment are not supported by research studies.

3. Three Minute Therapy encourages self-reliance and individual autonomy, while AA encourages each member to rely on the group, for example, by each member having another member as "sponsor" and guide.

4. Three Minute Therapy acknowledges the power of the individual to drink or not to drink. Whether an individual drinks or not is governed by that individual's beliefs, which can be changed. By contrast, AA disseminates the unfounded myth that individual "alcoholics" are "powerless" in the face of their "illness."

5. Three Minute Therapy aims to help people avoid addiction to therapy or to recovery meetings. AA offers the "alcoholic" no alternative to meetings and yet more meetings, until death parts the member from the AA church.

6. Three Minute Therapy always points out that the root of our drinking problem lies not in a disease, nor in our dysfunctional families, nor in

our addicted parents, nor in our "codependent" partners, but in our *beliefs*. (We invent and maintain these beliefs all by ourselves, though we may receive encouragement from our irrationally-minded families, friends, and partners.) AA does not expose these fallacies, but rather tends to reinforce them.

7. Three Minute Therapy attacks "musty" thinking and teaches clear thinking, whereas AA is an active disseminator of muddled and "musty" thinking.

## 12

## *Social Anxiety: To Hug and Hug Not*

*If you are reluctant to ask the way, you will be lost.*
—MALAY PROVERB

Whenever she met friends or acquaintances socially, Hilda faced an agonizing dilemma—to hug or not to hug. She couldn't think of any clear rule of etiquette governing hugging, and was afraid that people might disapprove of her if she were to hug or not hug when the opposite was judged more appropriate.

Hilda would even worry about this "difficult" decision ahead of time. "I can't very well hug Joanna, but wouldn't I insult her if I hugged Leslie and not her? I didn't hug Felicity the last couple of times—she didn't seem to want to—so wouldn't she think it strange if I were to hug her tonight? Do I know Rosemary well enough to hug her—or should I perhaps give her the opportunity to initiate the hugging?"

Hilda's hugging horror was just one of several predicaments she had created for herself. It's quite typical of a very widespread problem—anxiety about social interaction.

When Hilda first came to see me, she radiated nervousness and painful shyness. She positioned herself uncomfortably at the edge of my office's honey-yellow chair. She blurted out short, disjointed sentences, each somewhat disconnected from what preceded or followed. She punctuated her thoughts with a nervous giggle and a brief glance at me with restless eyes. Yet it wasn't difficult to see beyond this demeanor to a woman alive with energy and intelligence.

Hilda's wavy blonde hair and strong jaw betokened her Pennsylvania Dutch background. Just 21 years old, she was a college sophomore, determined to pursue a career in mathematics or physics. She aptly labeled herself "a bundle of nervous energy."

Hilda had already diagnosed her problem as "low self-esteem—withdrawing in social situations." Detailing a variety of her fears, she described a life of walking on thin ice, about to fall into the abyss below.

## Anxiety and Groups

Insecurity, awkwardness, and feeling out of place in social groups were a few of Hilda's numerous shyness-related symptoms. "My heart races—I feel faint, as if I'm going to black out. I'm afraid to say anything—I'm scared I will become the center of attention and then look like a fool," she gasped.

Recently, a college friend invited her and some mutual acquaintances to a dinner party. She was nervous beforehand, and once there Hilda was painfully aware of clamming up, feeling rigid, and remaining silent. She became self-conscious about this and forced herself to say one or two things. She was nervous that the others would talk much more than she would. She kept a running count of how many times everyone spoke and felt intense embarrassment that she uttered the fewest words.

"Suppose, Hilda," I asked, "that you actually did say less than everyone else, as you maintain. What's the worst aspect of this?"

"I dunno." She fluttered nervously.

"Project yourself back into that situation. Assume everyone's thinking about how quiet you are, which they're usually not—they're probably worried about how they're coming across. But anyway, let's grant you the worst-case scenario, that they're all thinking about you, you, you. So?"

"Well, who would want to be with someone who never talks?"

"Since you do have friends, apparently there are people who value your company. But the main issue is that you're *demanding* that you talk. You have yourself convinced that if you don't it would be the end of the universe, and that you'd turn into a worm. And then when you put that kind of pressure on yourself, you clam up and talk even less!" "Yes—I see what you're saying."

The next step was to help Hilda identify and then dispute the "musts" that were creating all this mischief. We came up with the following:

- I MUST be liked by others or else I'm unlikable

- I MUST prove I'm competent socially or else I'm no good

- I MUST show how bright I am or else I'm a dummy

- I MUST not appear different or else I'm a pariah

- I MUST not act stupid or else I'm an idiot

- I MUST avoid being the center of attention and it's awful if I stand out

I recommended that Hilda use a technique employing flashcards. First I asked her to write each of these "musts" on one side of an index card. We then devised some rational alternatives to each statement and put it on the other side. We tried to write at least four or five statements on the reverse side in response to each irrational belief. For example in response to "I MUST be liked by others or else I'm unlikable," some of the rational alternatives consisted of:

1. Although I prefer to be liked by others, I don't absolutely HAVE TO be!

2. The dislike of others is unpleasant but never horrible, terrible, or awful!

3. Some people disliking me does not prove that other people won't like me!

4. Even if no one ever liked me (which could hardly happen if I continue to put myself out and meet people) I could still fully accept myself!

5. Although friendships consists of one way to enjoy life, without them there are still practically an infinite number of other ways to enjoy life, including work, hobbies, long-term projects, and momentary pleasures!

6. Rejection by others in no way proves I'm a worthless person, but rather is just an indication of their taste!

7. It's not the rejection by others that gives me low self-esteem, but rather its my own self-condemnation about this rejection that does this!

She would carry the index cards with her and look at a few of them whenever she had a few seconds: waiting on line at the store, waiting for the bus, while eating, while on hold, and during commercials while watching TV. This was a convenient and time-saving way for her to practice rational thinking.

I suggested to her that she always write out a Three Minute Exercise immediately before meeting friends.

## *Hilda's Three Minute Exercise*

We targeted her belief, "I MUST appear to do the right thing in the right way when greeting." Here is one of the many Three Minute Exercises Hilda did to help her with this worry:

A. (**A**ctivating event): What if other people think I am hugging the wrong people, or not hugging the right people, or showing my awkwardness by being indecisive about hugging someone?

B. (irrational **B**elief): I MUST appear poised, savvy, and appropriate regarding who, how, and when I hug.

C. (emotional **C**onsequences): Anxiety.

D. (**D**isputing): What is the evidence I MUST appear poised, savvy, and appropriate regarding who, how, and when I hug?

E. (**E**ffective new thinking): No such evidence exists. Since I'm an imperfect human, I will not always appear poised and suave. If my friends think badly of me, that's sad, not the end of the universe. I can stand their disapproval. I've greeted people imperfectly in the past and it wasn't awful. I will in the future and I'll survive.

The more I push myself to hug, the more comfortable I'll tend to get at it, although I may never feel perfectly comfortable about it. Some of my friends probably feel a bit awkward about this also but they survive, and usually don't appear terribly uncomfortable.

It's not the awkwardness or anything else about my greeting or their reaction to it that makes me anxious, but rather it's my self-created demand that it go well that's the fundamental cause of my anxiety. I can change how I view it and thereby make myself considerably less anxious even if my interactions don't improve. The logical extension of my fear is that the whole world boycotts me because they don't like the way I hug, but that prospect just seems very humorous!

F. (new **F**eeling): Concern, rather than anxiety, about other people's possible disapproval of me.

## Paradoxical Intention

Hilda had another social fear that was more unusual. It arose when she was in a quiet setting, such as a movie during hushed scenes, the soft passages in a classical music concert, or when in bed with her boyfriend. She worried that she might swallow loudly and others might hear this each time she swallowed. She feared that they would think her weird, recognize she was anxious, self-conscious, or uncomfortable and thus find her annoying or be disdainful of her.

For Hilda I proposed a technique called *Paradoxical Intention*, formulated by the Viennese psychiatrist Viktor Frankl. Frankl related the true story of a man afflicted by a severe case of stuttering. This man couldn't remember an occasion when he had ever been able to speak without stuttering—except just once, when he was 12 years old. He had hooked a ride on a streetcar, and was caught by the conductor. The 12-year-old decided to play for sympathy by deliberately stuttering in order to depict himself as a poor, inadequate boy who was not worth prosecuting. But at that very moment, when he was deliberately trying to stutter, he found that he spoke normally and didn't stutter. Frankl developed this idea as a therapeutic technique: When his clients had some behavior from which they wished to refrain, Frankl would ask them to deliberately strive to engage in just that behavior.

I recommended to Hilda, when she started to worry about swallowing loud, that she say to herself: "I'll try to show my date what a noisy swallower I am. I will try to swallow as loudly as I possibly can, louder than anyone has ever swallowed!"

This technique required the kind of sense of humor that allows one to laugh at one's flaws. At times Hilda possessed perspective and she found the paradoxical intention helpful. She discovered that when she tried really hard to swallow noisily, she was unable to make much noise by swallowing and lost her self-consciousness. She reported that, as a result of practicing paradoxical intention, she developed an entirely new perspective on noisy swallowing: "It's not awful or horrible if I do this, in fact it's kind of humorous!"

Hilda continued to work conscientiously at the paradoxical intention, the Three Minute Therapy written exercises, and the index cards. Her strong commitment to practice these strategies daily never flagged. Predictably, her hard work resulted in diminishing social anxiety. By her third session, she would commence by excitedly relating the past week's progress.

## The Happy Hugger

As well as her Emotional Problem of social anxiety, Hilda did have a Practical Problem—in certain social situations she was unsure of the "correct" way to behave. I encouraged her to do research in this area. For instance, in the case of hugging, she wrote to an advice column enquiring about the etiquette of hugging. She also began to keep a notebook recording other people's hugging behavior and drew some conclusions about the "right," or at least the most popular, occasions to hug.

However, I also recommended to Hilda that she immediately begin to follow the guideline: "When in doubt, hug." An excellent rule of thumb in dealing with social anxiety is to do whatever's more out of character for you. Acting according to this principle enables a person to prove in practice that the feared course of action doesn't lead to the end of the world. Furthermore, people generally respond favorably to friendly behavior. If someone hugs more than is customary, people rarely think badly of that person for hugging. Instead, they instinctively like that person who seems to show by her hugging that she cares about them and thinks them important.

During Hilda's ninth session, it became obvious to me that I was about to lose a client. I congratulated Hilda on this fact.

## He's So Shy

Bob was 51. He spoke in a low, barely audible whisper, looking up not more than twice during our entire forty-five-minute session.

With much feeling he told me about his background: "I had a dysfunctional childhood and I've had fears all my life. My father left when I was five years old so I was raised by my mother along with two brothers and two sisters. My mother scolded me piercingly when I was growing up. She put in overtime criticizing me; she was always cold, never showing love and affection. I was petrified of her criticism so I played the role of the good, ever-obedient child. I tried so hard to guess what she was thinking so that I wouldn't displease her."

"My fears and shyness have something to do with the pain in my childhood. That's why I'm so afraid of criticism and lack self-esteem. I need approval. I don't have any good friends because I'm afraid to open up and expose myself. And I don't say much at the office."

## Not A Victim

I commiserated with Bob over his painful childhood and neurotic mother but quickly emphasized that he was mistaken about the causes of his current problems. Although his mother was responsible for her ill treatment of him, it was Bob himself who was now responsible for his fears. He perpetuated them and kept them alive.

Bob somewhat reluctantly admitted that the notion that he was not a helpless victim of his upbringing was appealing to him. It was clear, however, that he was unwilling to immediately abandon his pop-Freudian mythology lock, stock, and barrel.

"It's hard to argue with your clear, logical perspective. The idea that, in short order, I can eliminate hurts, troubles, and damage that I've harbored for my entire life leaves me with a mix of hope and skepticism. I guess I should try it before I decide it's too good to be true."

## Understanding Shyness

Social anxiety is often described as "shyness," but many people who don't consider themselves shy experience interactions with other people as uncomfortable or awkward. Around 40 percent of the American population describe themselves as "shy," while a vast majority admit to having been shy at some time in their lives. Some people go through an extremely shy phase in childhood or adolescence and later emerge from this. One client of mine, a person of extremely self-confident demeanor, related the story of his first early love interest at the age of eleven. Both he and the girl were so acutely shy that, whenever they were alone together, neither one would say a word to the other. So although they were going together for several months, they never spoke to each other except when other people were present!

We readily use the term "shy" for those people who shrink from social interaction and whose manner is timid, yet it is well-known that many forceful, even flamboyant figures are "shy underneath," and some even claim that their shyness drives them to their attention-catching behavior. Among celebrities who have confessed to being shy are Barbara Walters, Johnny Mathis, Carol Burnett, Bob Dole, John Cleese, opera star Joan Sutherland, David Niven, Rush Limbaugh, Conan O'Brien, and Kim Basinger. Some celebrities, like Garrison Keillor and the notoriously flamboyant trial lawyer Melvin Belli, have stated that they entered upon their careers precisely because of their shyness.

Shy people will often inconvenience themselves to an extreme degree to avoid human encounters. ATMs (cash dispensers) have saved some shy people from the dreaded prospect of having to talk to a human bank teller, though the extremely shy person will probably wait until no one else is near the ATM until he uses it, fearful that spectators would form derogatory judgments about his ineptitude with the machine.

Shy people will often fail to assert themselves or even to ask simple questions when it would be to their advantage. They may spend hours driving around lost because they are too intimidated to stop and ask someone for directions. When they do engage in conversation, they will sometimes lose valuable opportunities because their panicky feelings deflect them from seeking answers which would help them. Often, a shy person's anxious behavior may be interpreted by other people as unfriendliness.

Another disadvantage of shyness is often overlooked. Shy people may be over-inclined to agree with anyone to whom they are talking because they dread that person's disapproval. They will sometimes agree to things they would prefer not to agree to, because they are afraid other people will think badly of them if they resist their suggestions. Sometimes socially anxious people feel able to break from this pattern of compliance only by becoming angry. People in this predicament can reduce both their shyness and their anger by daily Three Minute Exercises. And they can address their *Practical* Problem (lack of skill in social encounters, and a habit of agreeing too easily) by observing other people and experimenting with various behaviors.

Manipulative individuals such as con-men and cult leaders are often expert at using the fears of the shy and socially anxious to create converts. The manipulator is able to convey to the dupe that she need have no fear of social awkwardness as long as she goes along with the manipulator's schemes. Freedom from uncomfortable social interaction seems to lie in eagerly embracing the outlook and objectives of the manipulator. Women who have fears about their social skills are often pressured into relationships by such techniques, and sometimes even find themselves married to a particular individual for no better reason than that he was able, whether consciously or by instinct, to play upon the woman's social anxiety. A series of encounters in which the woman did not summon up the courage to say "No" may lead to a major legal and domestic entanglement.

Some therapists say that shyness can be a good thing. But this confuses emotion with behavior. It can certainly be useful to adopt a somewhat reserved, quiet manner, and this will make you a more attractive person than the crude loudmouth. But it is possible to act quiet and reserved as a matter of choice, without the emotional pains of shyness and without wasting one's brainpower on endless preoccupation with one's own social shortcomings.

Another associated problem is that social anxiety often prompts individuals to overuse drugs like alcohol, which are consumed to excess in an attempt to reduce the agony of awkward social interaction or to improve performance in social situations.

There is accumulating evidence that shyness is partly genetic in origin. This doesn't mean that nothing can be done about the problems caused by shyness. It is genetically determined that when you jump into a swimming pool there is an immediate chilling sensation, which it is natural to avoid as a highly unpleasant shock. But someone who wants to swim regularly soon overcomes this problem and learns to put up with the immediate chill for the sake of the subsequent enjoyment. In time the enthusiastic swimmer may come to reinterpret the chill itself as a bracing experience to be welcomed.

Similarly with shyness. One can train oneself to "break the ice" and become engaged in relaxed conversations, even if one is naturally shy.

## Three Minute Relaxation

Due to his apprehension generated by his deeply ingrained "musts," Bob felt tense and nervous almost all of the time. Consequently, in addition to teaching him many of the exercises discussed in earlier chapters, I taught him a general progressive relaxation strategy.

I taught Bob *Three Minute Relaxation* in my office and then recommended that he practice it at home. It eventually became a useful adjunctive technique for him. He used it to fall asleep and to treat his anxious symptoms when he was feeling stressed out at work.

It might seem that a relaxation technique is contrary to the theme of this book, since it does not directly address the sufferer's *thinking*. However, relaxation is a partial solution to the *practical* problem of tension and awkwardness associated with shyness. It directly attacks the physical and emotional *effects* of the sufferer's "musty" thinking and is thus able to provide some relief from distress, pending the complete removal of the problem. Relaxation exercises have the additional benefit that they serve as a distraction from the problem by giving the sufferer something else to think about; they therefore help to reduce secondary anxiety (see chapter 13).

I suggested Bob record the relaxation exercises on his phone. Next I asked him to find a comfortable position in his chair, then close his eyes. I engaged the tape recorder, and repeated these instructions:

"Now, Bob, focus on your feet and ankles (Pause). Notice any tightness or any tension anywhere in your feet and ankles (Pause). Now feel all that tightness and all that tension flow right out (Pause). Your feet and ankles are getting heavier and heavier, more and more relaxed (Pause). Relax (Pause). Relax (Pause). Relax (Pause).

I continued, naming each of the following muscle groups in order, while repeating the same instructions:

1. Lower legs and calves,

2. Upper legs and thighs,

3. Buttocks and hips,

4. Abdomen and pelvis,

5. Low back,

6. Upper back,

7. Chest and shoulders,

8. Arms and hands,

9. Neck and throat,

10. Jaw, face, and forehead,

11. Back and top of your head.

I concluded by having Bob repeat the same procedure used for individual muscle groups, but now focused on his entire body:

"Now focus on your entire body (Pause). Notice any tightness or any tension anywhere in your entire body (Pause). Now feel all that tightness and all that tension flow right out (Pause). Your entire body is getting heavier and heavier, more and more relaxed (Pause). Relax (Pause). Relax (Pause). Relax.

For the first three weeks, practicing once every day, it took Bob about twenty minutes to get results. Once he had mastered it, though, he was able to relax in about three minutes, concentrating primarily on the final step involving his entire body.

At the end of treatment Bob told me: "I had no idea this was really possible. Having had this problem for a lifetime with nothing to help it, I decided I had to learn to live with it." Then he added an intriguing remark: "You know, even though I didn't think this was possible, I always dreamed of this day when I would be free of the demons!"

## *Public Speaking Phobia*

Orren did not seem outwardly shy and did not admit to being inwardly shy. His bright smile, his colorful, casual dress, and his nonchalant posture all helped to place him in the least shy ten percent of the population. Yet, like so many people, shy and non-shy alike, Orren suffered from a terror of one particular kind of social intercourse—speaking in front of groups of people. The larger the group, the greater the terror for Orren, but even an audience of six was enough to make the speech an ordeal for him.

In his job as a financial advisor, Orren saw opportunities where he could get more clients and advance his career by making presentations to groups large and small. And he really loved talking, explaining his ideas on investments to clients or anyone interested. But the very thought of the horrors of addressing a group made his stomach churn with anxiety.

"I remember having a terrible fear of public speaking in the ninth grade. In my junior high school English class the teacher had each student in turn stand and read from *Macbeth.* As my turn approached, I could feel my heart pounding, and I felt I was about to throw up. Then the class was ended early because of a fire drill, just before it was my turn to read aloud. Maybe there was a God after all!

"That was Friday, so I was off the hook until Monday. All weekend my anxiety heightened. All I could think of was making a fool of myself while all eyes were fixed on me. Sunday night I hardly slept and Monday morning I was sick to my stomach. I lacked the faith to trust to another miracle, so I stayed home from school. When I went in on Tuesday, the class had finished reading from *Macbeth.*

"In college I put off taking the required speech class until my last term of my senior year. Each morning, before making a presentation, I felt as if I were on death row the morning I would be walked into the gas chamber. Once the talk was over, I would always experience enormous relief, as if I had been reprieved from execution.

"I worked out many ways of escaping from being called on to speak in class. Most of the time, though, sitting all the way in the back of the room and avoiding the teacher's eye seemed to work OK."

## *Orren's Three Minute Exercise*

Orren and I first tackled his public speaking phobia with a Three Minute Exercise:

A.  (**A**ctivating Event): I get up to speak in front of a group. I feel panicky, and I believe my nervousness is observable. Suppose that because of my anxiety I stutter, stammer, become incoherent, my mind goes blank so that I can't think of anything to say. People would then have a low opinion of me.

B.  (irrational **B**elief): I MUST not be thought badly of by the audience.

C.  (emotional **C**onsequences): I'm terrified.

D.  (**D**isputing): What's the evidence that I MUST not be thought badly of by the audience?

E.  (**E**ffective new thinking): There's just no evidence for the "must"—I will not magically turn into a worthless person if the audience should disapprove of me for one poor performance. What's the worst that could happen? A few people would have a lower opinion of me, and I might find it more difficult to get invited for future talks. That would be unfortunate, but not horrible or awful.

If they disdain me because of my behavior in the talk, this disdain does not change me; I'll be the same person as before, with or without their disdain. Their thoughts are just in their heads and can't reach out to grab me. Other people's condemnatory thoughts have the same effect on me as do the winds on Mars, blowing the Martian sand over the Martian rocks— absolutely none.

Experiencing anxiety and not always pleasing other people are inevitable and universal features of all human life. I will experience anxiety and arouse disapproval in other people's heads many times in my life—this is to be expected because we're all human. If I stammer and become incoherent on one occasion, this is unfortunate, but not a sentence of death.

If I work at it, I can learn to accept myself fully and get considerable enjoyment out of life, despite the unpleasant reality of occasional anxiety and disapproval, just as I can survive and prosper despite the unpleasant reality of occasionally catching a cold.

F. (new **F**eeling): Keen concern rather than terror.

## *Three Minute Imagery*

Three Minute Imagery, which we looked at in chapter 8, is a particularly good technique for problems like public speaking anxiety, which arise in situations faced infrequently. Three Minute Imagery can create a "virtual" public speaking situation within which to practice. Here is the Three Minute Imagery Orren did with my help:

## STEP 1

Vividly picture the worst possible thing you can imagine happening—in this case you get up to speak and appear very anxious. As a result of your anxiety, you stutter and stammer and your mind goes blank. And the audience condemns you for this.

## STEP 2

As you distinctly imagine this, allow yourself— right now in your gut—to get in touch with some feelings of terror about it.

## STEP 3

Still picturing the scene described in Step 1, make yourself feel only concerned and regretful, but not terrified. Since you create and control your own feelings, with persistence you can modify them. How do you make yourself feel concerned and regretful rather than terrified? Show yourself that you don't turn into a worm if the audience disapproves of you for poor performance. Remind yourself that at the very worst, there will be disadvantages, such as not being invited back to give future talks. Convince yourself by reasoned persuasion that although it can be highly pleasurable to receive other people's acceptance and appreciation, just as it can be pleasurable to win a lottery, no one's approval is a dire necessity. (At this point Orren added several other "rational" statements about disapproval and anxiety.)

As homework, Orren did this Three Minute Imagery for three minutes twice a day. He began with Steps 1 and 2, and once "in touch" with the emotions in Step 2 he immediately moved to Step 3. Orren's Three Minute Imagery overlapped with his Three Minute Exercise and reinforced it. If you find it difficult to devise a Three Minute Imagery that fits your case, begin with a Three Minute Exercise, and then base the imagery on the same A, B, and C.

Using his Three Minute Exercise and Three Minute Imagery, Orren was able to reduce his public speaking anxiety. Having done this, he found the motivation to join Toastmasters, a nationwide practice and self-help group for people who make speeches and other public presentations. This enabled him to tackle his practical problem of poorly developed public speaking skills. By attacking public speaking on both fronts, emotional and practical, Orren became an accomplished public speaker who experienced very little anxiety and soon grew to love speaking in public as much as he enjoyed speaking to a couple of friends in a bar. Within eighteen months, his attitude to public speaking had changed so much that he always looked forward eagerly to his next public speaking engagement. His public presentations gave him a threefold reward: they expanded his business, gave him an opportunity to indulge his usually sociable and talkative proclivities, and provided him satisfaction from knowing the progress he was making in overcoming an emotional problem he had once believed all-powerful and eternal.

# 13

## Secondary Disturbance: Getting Upset about Being Upset

> *I am always with myself, and it is I who am my tormentor.*
>
> —LEO TOLSTOY (1828–1910)

You are offered a million dollars to spend the night in a spooky "haunted" castle. If you're like most people, you would probably accept this offer with feelings of excited anticipation. You'd correctly rate as close to zero any risk of your experiencing a serious scare, but even if you saw, larger than life, a headless ghost with clanking chains you would very likely think hard about the million dollars and stay put.

But now suppose that, as part of this deal, you are connected to a "fear meter"—an electronic device to measure your heartbeat, perspiration, and other bodily signs of fear. If your level of fear rises above a certain point, as indicated by a needle on the fear meter dial, you lose.

Now, the proposition looks less attractive. If you did accept it, you might start worrying more about what was showing on the fear meter dial than about what the ghosts could do to you. With every creepy creak of a door, your thoughts might instantly turn to the needle on that dial, and you might have the thought, *Am I going to lose this bet because I am having a twinge of fear?* The knowledge that you could lose the bet because of a high fear reading might cause you to lose the bet. You would be more fearful about your fear than about the ghosts!

Although I have invented a fanciful example to illustrate the point, this is a very common problem of everyday life, a problem called "secondary disturbance." In fact, the majority of people with emotional problems undergo some kind of secondary disturbance. Yet, it is a problem that most traditional therapists have completely ignored.

An adolescent boy introduced to the girl of his dreams blushes, and then feels like a fool *because he is blushing*. He is embarrassed about being embarrassed.

A busy executive lies awake in bed worrying about deadlines. As he becomes aware that he is not dropping off to sleep, he starts to worry that he is going to be awake all night. *This worry then preys on his mind and keeps him awake*. He is staying awake because of his fear of staying awake.

A political speech writer who puts herself down at every opportunity, with consequent bouts of depression, begins to think: "What a worthless creep I am; I'm always depressed." *This thought does nothing to cheer her up*. She becomes further depressed about being depressed.

Sometimes the secondary disturbance is a different emotion from the primary disturbance. A woman turns down a job because it involves taking a glass elevator to the 30th floor every day, and she experiences fear at the thought of this. *She then becomes ashamed of her fear,* and potentially depressed about it. She is depressed about her fear of heights

Notice that such cases are even more unreasonable than the haunted castle example. In that illustration, being afraid could lead to losing a chance of acquiring a million dollars. No such heavy stakes are usually involved in everyday examples of secondary disturbance, but when people observe that they are distraught, they often give themselves a hard time about it. They do this because they place a demand upon themselves. They tell themselves, "I MUST not become distraught. I SHOULD remain cool and in control at all times."

## *Fearing Fear Itself*

Lynn appeared at my office door, a tall, willowy figure with a bounce in her step, sporting shoulder-length auburn hair. She looked a good ten years younger than her actual age of 43, and wore an infectious smile, highlighted by her large, coal-black sparkling eyes.

Lynn had recently landed a position as managing editor of a national women's magazine, and with her emerald velvet pants and white trim blouse, she looked every inch the part. Deeply in love with her work, she stated that she worried "too much" about getting fired. Early in our first session, her desperation became apparent.

"I start worrying when a deadline's approaching. As it nears I get more and more nervous. Then I start blocking, and my project's almost always late. It becomes obvious that I'm the nutcase of the office. I just GOTTA stop being so uptight," she concluded.

"You really have two emotional problems, not just one," I pointed out.

"*Two* emotional problems?"

"Yes. First you make yourself anxious about the deadline."

"Yeah, that's my problem."

"That's your initial problem. But when you notice this anxiety, you then make yourself anxious about *that,*" I explained.

"You mean I'm anxious *about* being anxious?"

"Precisely."

"Oh no, that's awful!" she exclaimed (ready to become anxious about being anxious about being anxious).

"It's not really awful. But it *is* two problems. First your anxiety about your practical difficulties—meeting the deadline. And second, your anxiety *about* your anxiety. But both problems are soluble," I assured Lynn.

"Really? *Really?* How can I solve them?"

"Well, you can start by attending to the Secondary Problem, your anxiety *about* your anxiety. Once you've eliminated that, you can then think more clearly about your primary anxiety and surrender that too."

I sometimes humorously tell my clients that Franklin Delano Roosevelt had a secondary disturbance problem. He said: "The only thing we have to fear is fear itself." Of course, that was just a figure of speech, but it does illustrate the way people take for granted the false belief that the only way to avoid something is to be worked up emotionally about it.

## Free-Floating Folly

Traditional therapists would label Lynn's secondary problem "free-floating anxiety," the result of unconscious forces and childhood conflicts, not tied to anything in the present.

This notion, largely popularized by Freudians and post-Freudians, is mistaken. There exists no emotion—anxiety or any other—that is truly "free-floating." Anxiety is anchored in specific irrational beliefs in relation to specific circumstances. By their use of the term "free-floating," traditional therapists reveal their failure to understand that feelings are governed by thinking, and that emotional problems are most often the outcome of "musty" or demanding thoughts.

## Ego Disturbance vs. Discomfort Disturbance

As we have observed, secondary disturbance arises because the individual is disturbed *about* being disturbed. The individual thinks: "I MUST not get disturbed. For me to be disturbed is just horrible." But what is it about the original disturbance that the individual finds so unacceptable? Here we observe two distinct possibilities: *ego disturbance* and *discomfort disturbance*.

In ego disturbance the person thinks: "If I get upset, if I become fearful or anxious or depressed, it shows that I am an inadequate or seriously flawed person. It shows that I am no good, worthless, a failure."

In discomfort disturbance the individual thinks: "If I get upset, or if I become fearful, anxious, or depressed, this is a dreadful, intolerable feeling. I cannot stand to undergo such anguish."

As you will recall from Chapter 1, ego disturbance is "Must" #1 (demand on oneself), while discomfort disturbance is "Must" #3 (demand on the Universe).

## Lynn's Ego

The first step in attacking Lynn's secondary anxiety was to diagnose it as either an ego or a discomfort disturbance.

Lynn was putting herself down for feeling uptight. She was telling herself: "I MUST not be so disturbed, and when I am, this proves that I'm a weak *person.*" Lynn was able to see that becoming anxious was a human weakness, but paradoxically, she wished to forbid herself to be human and have that weakness. Lynn had an ego disturbance. Here's one of the Three Minute Exercises she wrote out to combat her underlying "must":

## *Lynn's Three Minute Exercise*

A. (**A**ctivating event): I'm making myself very up-tight about this deadline.

B. (irrational **B**elief): I MUST not make myself up-tight. If I do, it proves that I'm a weak person.

C. (emotional **C**onsequence): Anxiety about my anxiety.

D. (**D**isputing): Why MUST I not make myself up-tight?

E. (**E**ffective new thinking): There's no reason why I MUST not make myself nervous about a deadline. I prefer not to, and it's unfortunate that I do. Making myself anxious is a human weakness, something that all humans do, and hardly turns me into a weak person. It would be better for me to fully accept myself, no matter what, even when I'm nervous.

At worst, I could continue to make myself nervous about deadlines for the rest of my life, and not get such good jobs as I would like. That would prove rather uncomfortable, but would hardly rate as a horror. Even if I always have this problem, there's no reason why I can't be fairly happy, if I just accept myself as imperfect. There's no reason why I couldn't accomplish tasks when anxious, though not as well as if I were not upset.

Furthermore, just because I have this problem, it doesn't follow that I will always have it. I'm an ongoing process and forever changing. So if I conscientiously practice my Three Minute Exercises, why couldn't I beat it? I damn well could!

I intend to keep working on this problem until I beat it. Accomplishing this is largely a matter of repetition and reinforcement. Many others make themselves nervous about deadlines, but even if I were the only one with this problem, it would be no more than a pain in the ass—not awful, terrible, or horrible.

F. (new **F**eeling): Concern, rather than anxiety, about the initial anxiety.

## *Afraid to Ask*

Here's another example of secondary anxiety, taken from my monthly advice column, "Ask Dr. Mike":

DEAR DR. MIKE: Recently, while chatting with an attractive woman at a party, I decided I wanted to see her again and thought of asking for her phone number. Immediately, my heart started racing, and I couldn't bring myself to ask for her number. I dragged the conversation on for quite a while, hoping that I would calm down enough to ask for her number. Does this experience mean that I'm afraid of commitment?

—NUMBERLESS

DEAR NUMBERLESS: Probably not. There is a much more simple and probable explanation—and it isn't a fear of numbers! Rather, you may have a problem usually overlooked by psychotherapists: *the fear of momentary anxiety.*

While chatting with her, you probably realized that it would feel a little awkward to change conversational gears and request her number (a little discomfort). Perhaps you recognized that she possibly might not be interested, and might therefore be put on the spot (a little more discomfort). Then you guessed that if she did reject you, you might feel disappointed and even faintly humiliated (yet a little more discomfort). Next, you might have projected that you'd be anxious about a little rejection (still more discomfort, and now some anxiety).

Finally, you might have told yourself: "All this discomfort and anxiety will prove AWFUL, TERRIBLE, and HORRIBLE. I CANNOT face it. I MUST avoid it." And so you missed out on a possible relationship.

The solution begins with recognizing that a change in view results in a change in behavior, so adopt the following hardheaded (but open-hearted) view: "No excuses and no debates. I'm going to ask for her number right now if it's the last thing I do. If it kills me, it kills me. Since I abhor discomfort and anxiety, I had better face it immediately and thereby create more comfort for myself in the long run." Then ruthlessly take the plunge.

This strategy will help you keep the immediate discomfort and anxiety in its proper perspective. A delightful, long-term relationship may well follow.

## *Depression About Anxiety*

At first glance, Elmer had a carefree appearance. As he sat down across from me, he whistled through his front teeth while precipitously dangling a matchstick from the right corner of his mouth. Wearing tight, faded jeans and a half-unbuttoned plaid flannel shirt, Elmer's sleeves were rolled up to reveal brimming muscles. A straw hat and cowboy boots seemed somehow missing.

# Secondary Disturbance

Elmer's problem was a fear of crowds and of waiting in line. So he avoided restaurants, movies, theaters, and parties. He also worried about doing badly in his work as a commercial artist.

Elmer felt relaxed only at home with his lover, Chuck, yet he was beginning to feel guilty even with him. Elmer blamed himself because Chuck had chosen to restrict his social life drastically in order to spend all his free time with Elmer.

Because of these pervasive fears, Elmer felt depressed. Only Chuck, who came with Elmer on his first visit to me, knew about his problems.

"I shouldn't have these silly fears," he told me. "It embarrasses me to think how weak I am."

"How does it make you weak to be human and have fears?" I asked.

"It just does. It's not as if I get afraid once in a while. These fears dominate my life. I'm not strong enough to face them."

"It sounds as if you think you're either a *strong* person or a *weak* person."

"Yeah, I guess you could say that. I used to think I was a strong person. But I'm sure a weakie now."

In Elmer's head he became a strong person when he dealt fearlessly with problems. Conversely, he thought he had turned into a "weakie" when he was beset by fears, as he often was of late. In reality, of course, Elmer was, like everyone else, a person who at times acts strongly and at other times acts weakly.

Elmer was, like Lynn, putting himself down because of his primary disturbance. By condemning himself for getting disturbed, Elmer was actually decreasing his chances of eliminating his fears. His conviction that he was a weak person set up a self-fulfilling prophecy:

1. Elmer, like all of us, has anxieties. He predicts they will not diminish (prophecy).

2. But Elmer incorrectly concludes that this makes him *a weak person* (self-downing).

3. As a *weak person*, he considers himself unable to act strongly and conquer his anxieties (hopelessness).

4. So he gives up facing his fears (avoidance).

5. Unaddressed, his fears grow stronger (fulfillment of the prophecy).

## *Seven Easy Steps*

Elmer and Lynn each condemned themselves for having Emotional Problems. They foolishly denigrated themselves for doing something that all humans do easily and naturally—get upset. Their self-condemnation created Secondary Problems worse than the primary problem itself.

Do you ever make statements condemning yourself? "What an idiot I am!" "Well, that's just the sort of blunder you'd expect from a klutz like me!" If you find it natural to condemn yourself in this way for mistakes, you probably also condemn yourself about any fears, anxieties, gloomy feelings you experience. But this only makes it harder to tackle your Primary Emotional Problem.

Here is a simple approach to dealing with your Secondary Problem:

1. *Specify your upset emotion.* Try to identify your Primary Problem. Is it anxiety, depression, guilt, or hostility?

2. *Determine whether there's a Secondary Problem.* Are you upsetting yourself about that initial upsetness?

    A general anxiety or depression that seems to materialize "out of the blue," not directly related to anything concrete in your life, is a clue. In all probability, it really is related to something specific—your experience of feeling anxious or depressed about some Practical Problem. You are worried that you may get anxious— upset about being upset.

    Feeling overwhelmed, out of control, or as if you're going crazy is usually a sign that you have a Secondary Problem. You're feeling "out of control" because you feel unable to control your Primary Emotional Problem, and you think you "must" control it.

    For instance, a client of mine says: "Work is really getting me down. I feel overwhelmed. I just can't face it." But what is really the object of her feeling overwhelmed is the foreboding she has when she goes to work in the morning or the panic that arises when she thinks about the pile of papers on her desk.

3. *Identify your "musts."* What are you telling yourself that creates your secondary problem? "I MUST not be anxious, or else I'm an inadequate person." "I MUST not keep depressing myself about the same situations, because if I do, it makes me a hopeless case." "I MUST not be nervous and awkward, because if I am, people will notice, and I could not stand that."

4. *Challenge your "musts."* If your friend believes in Santa Claus, and you tell him "There is no Santa Claus," you have expressed your opinion, but you have not really *challenged* or effectively *disputed* his belief.

But instead you might say to your friend: "What's your evidence for the existence of Santa? Give me some facts to support your contention. Prove it to me." Now you're pushing him to defend his belief. This encourages him to actively question its truth.

Use this same challenging approach with yourself: "What's the evidence I MUST not be anxious? Where is it written that I become a hopelessly weak person because I sometimes act weakly? Prove I CAN'T STAND people thinking I'm nervous."

5. *Refute your "musts."* Don't be satisfied with facile answers. Think it through carefully and see if you can come up with evidence to support the "must." Discover that there's really no evidence for the demands that underlie your "musty" thinking. A "must" implies that there's an absolute law of the universe that you "ought" not to be upset. Obviously, there can be no such law, or you wouldn't be upset.

Clearly, it's *preferable* that you do not upset yourself. It's *desirable* to avoid anxiety. But we're not debating what is preferable or desirable—we're debating your "must."

When you act weakly or irrationally, we cannot conclude that your *entire self* is weak and irrational. At times, like all humans, you act irrationally and at times you act rationally.

6. *Take risks.* You can convince yourself, *in action,* that you're not a wholly weak and inadequate person. You can actively court "danger"—seek out situations in which you become upset. Avoidance only helps to *reinforce* your secondary fears.

If you get panicky in elevators and are telling yourself you're inadequate and a loser for this weakness, go out of your way to take an elevator.

If, like many new parents, you easily become angry at your young children and feel like a loathsome failure because of this, seek out opportunities to be in your children's company just when they're at their most difficult.

If you feel anxious about committing yourself to intimate relationships, plunge into a relationship.

7. *Utilize practice and reinforcement.* Go through the steps outlined above many times. Resolutely launch a campaign to accept yourself thoroughly, with all your emotional problems. Have no fear that this will make you complacent about those problems, so that you fail to do anything about them! Quite the contrary, you will find that it is much easier to deal with problems if you don't get upset about the fact that you have them. The first step to achieving control over your upsets is to abandon the demand to have superhuman control of yourself.

Convince yourself, by argument and disputation, and also by observation and experiment, that becoming unnecessarily upset is a typical human weakness, and not something to which you can reasonably expect to be granted immunity.

## Anne's Discomfort Anxiety

Anne called me to cancel her first therapy appointment with only thirty minutes notice but with heartfelt apologies. She rescheduled for the following week and again failed to appear. When I did finally meet her, it soon came out that this pattern of unreliability pervaded her entire life.

After some questioning, I found that Anne suffered from acrophobia—fear of heights. She made herself extremely anxious about driving across bridges. Traveling to my office from her home meant crossing a bridge, as did traveling from her home to her office.

On occasional bad days, Anne would set out for work, turn around at the entry to the bridge, and return home. On fairly good days, Anne did make it across the bridge—but it took her an hour to cajole herself to cross. Every morning she allowed herself an hour and twenty minutes to get to work: twenty minutes to drive to work and one hour to get up the nerve to cross the three-quarter-mile bridge.

"I just fall apart when I try to cross that bridge," she explained.

"What do you mean by 'fall apart'?" I asked her.

"I start shaking all over. I can't catch my breath; I feel like jelly. I put it off as long as I can, then I decide I have to face it. So I clench my teeth, shut my eyes, and speed across. It's absolutely horrible."

"What aspect is horrible?"

"Those feelings. You have no idea how horrible they are. I feel like I'm going to die. No—it's worse. I feel as if something even worse than death is going to happen, but I don't know what. I feel as though I'm going crazy."

"You put off crossing the bridge as long as possible to avoid these very unpleasant feelings?"

"Yes—those feelings terrify me."

"I understand that it seems so. But in reality, it's never feelings that terrify you. It's always what you tell yourself about those feelings. Such as: 'Crossing the bridge SHOULDN'T be so unpleasant, I can't STAND shaking, It's HORRIBLE to feel like jelly.' "

"I don't understand."

"In reality, those feelings are extremely unpleasant. But if you were realistic, you'd cross the bridge as soon as possible to get it over with. You wouldn't agonize and prolong the discomfort."

"I never thought of it that way."

"But when you bring in the magical notions: 'It SHOULDN'T be so unpleasant, it's AWFUL, and I CAN'T STAND it,' then you make it feel much worse than it really is. And you extend the unpleasantness for an hour twice a day.

Anne was not suffering from ego disturbance. She did not think she was an unworthy person because she felt panicky crossing over bridges. But she had made herself afraid of those panicky feelings and told herself she could not tolerate them.

## *Applying Problem Separation To A Secondary Disturbance*

We have learned in earlier chapters that it's useful to separate a Practical Problem from an associated Emotional Problem: this is the Problem Separation Technique. We can now see that the same approach works for Primary and Secondary Emotional Problems. Just as people often think that their Practical Problem is *causing* their Primary Emotional Problem (A causing C), so they often think that their Primary Emotional Problem is *causing* their Secondary Emotional Problem.

To tackle your Secondary Problem, the best approach is to separate it from your Primary Problem. Then fully accept your Primary Problem, your initial disturbed feeling, so that you don't go on to disturb yourself *about* your disturbed feeling. Accepting your Primary Problem means that your desire to be rid of that problem is a *preference,* not a "must." Since "musts" generate Emotional Problems, feeling that you MUST rid yourself of your Primary Problem is likely to generate a new Emotional Problem—your Secondary Problem. This Secondary Problem tends to get in the way of tackling the Primary Problem.

It may seem paradoxical to *accept* your Primary disturbance, because you do want to remove that disturbance. But if you run over someone in your car, do you think it would be helpful to reverse the car and run over them again in the opposite direction? No, that would do nothing to heal the original injuries, would add new injuries, and would complicate the first injuries so that they were harder to treat. Having hurt yourself by inflicting your Primary disturbance on yourself, it will not help to inflict an additional disturbance by upsetting yourself *about* your Primary disturbance.

By *accepting* your disturbance, I don't mean accepting that there's nothing you can do about it. But simply accept that you do have that Primary disturbance, and that this is a typical human failing.

You are accepting your problem if:

- You believe that, although feeling upset is distinctly uncomfortable, it's an essential aspect of the human condition

- You see that, although such feelings detract from your enjoyment of life, they do not obliterate all of it

- You're aware that such unpleasant feelings tend to wax and wane

- You recognize that dwelling on them only tends to prolong and intensify them needlessly

- You know that it's best to face up to them rather than avoid them

You are hurting yourself, just as if you were hitting yourself on the head with a hammer, if:

- You tell yourself you can't stand feeling anxious or upset

- You believe that life is terrible because you're feeling down

- You tell yourself that life SHOULDN'T be so uncomfortable

- You regularly avoid situations just because you associate them with some emotional discomfort

## Secondary Disturbance

Once you have identified your Primary disturbance, classify your Secondary Disturbance. Are you upset about being upset? If you are, discover the beliefs that make you disturbed about your Primary disturbance. Are your putting yourself down (ego disturbance) or are you putting the Universe down (discomfort disturbance)? Either way, you can challenge and combat your unreasonable beliefs and change them. Then your Secondary Disturbance will evaporate, leaving you in a better position to tackle your Primary Disturbance.

# 14

## How to Be Happy: A Beginning

*Every journey of a thousand miles begins with a single step.*

—CHINESE PROVERB

Some years ago the scripts of the Monty Python TV comedy shows were released in book form under the title, *The Complete Works of Shakespeare and Monty Python. Volume I: Monty Python.* In the same spirit, we might have called this book *How to Become Happy, Wise, and Successful. Volume I: How to Stop Making Yourself Miserable.*

People often look for a sudden psychotherapeutic "cure," which will at one stroke guarantee their elevation to a higher plane of living, where there is no danger of being irrational, neurotic, or self-destructive. No such miracle cure exists.

This doesn't mean that lasting happiness is forever beyond your reach. But you're unlikely to attain it without some modest first steps, and as long as you fail to attain it, these modest first steps will still improve your life to some extent. If you're anxious or depressed, it's probably because you make yourself anxious or depressed by the way you think. Reading this book will put you on the road to being able to overcome your unhappiness by changing your thinking.

## *Achieving Your Goals*

Three Minute Therapy is a tool designed to help you become better at achieving your goals. It does not tell you what those goals should be. Whether you should have many children or remain childless, whether you should work hard and increase your money income or take things easier and retire with few savings, whether science is more important than art or religion—these are all questions this book does not try to answer.

Whatever your life's goals, you will be happier if they are motivated by preferences rather than by demands. You will be happier if you take practical, rational steps to attain your goals, while always accepting that you may fail to attain some of them.

If you have goals that are being frustrated by an emotional or behavioral problem, eliminating or diminishing that problem then becomes a goal for you. Thus, if one of your goals is to publish a novel, and your depression is slowing down your writing it, conquering your depression becomes in its turn a goal for you.

Most of the chapters in this book cover specific problems such as procrastination (a behavioral problem) or worry (an emotional problem). If you have such a problem, reread the corresponding chapter in this book several times and practice the recommended exercises. If your problem is not discussed specifically, you can still easily adapt the lessons of this book to fit your requirements.

Perhaps you have one of the following problems:

- You are unattached, and your goal is to meet a partner for companionship, sex, love, and marriage

- You are unhappy with your line of work and desire to move into a different field

- You have a sexual problem such as impotence or difficulty achieving orgasm

None of these problems is the subject of a chapter in this book. But you can analyze your problem by first applying the Problem Separation Technique (described in chapters 3, 4, and 5) to identify your practical problem and your emotional problem. Quite likely your emotional problem is discussed in this book. For example, if your practical problem is that you are unattached and long for a relationship, your emotional/behavioral problem may be social anxiety (discussed in chapter 12) or it may be procrastination (chapter 6).

If your particular problem is not covered in this book, you can still adapt Three Minute Therapy to your problem. You can devise your own Three Minute Exercises to combat any emotional or behavioral difficulty. In each case, you know that your emotional problem is a C. You identify the A, the Activating Event or situation, which triggers your C. You next determine your B—what you are telling yourself about A. Then at D you dispute your B— confront it, challenge it, question it. At E, you formulate the new, reasonable thinking which replaces your B. The result of writing out the Three Minute Exercise regularly and thoughtfully will be F—a better emotional state or a more effective behavior.

Of all forms of therapy, Three Minute Therapy is most easily adapted to eliminate the therapist, partially or completely. This book enables you to become your own therapist.

## *Some Common Objections to Three Minute Therapy*

1. *Don't we need to get at the childhood roots of personal problems?*

Emotional and behavioral problems do not have childhood roots. They have cognitive roots: it's your *present beliefs* which create your problem.

Even if you did accept and begin to act upon these beliefs when you were a child, those beliefs are harming you because you follow them *now. How* you came by your self-destructive ideas may be fascinating if you want to understand your life story, but it has no bearing on the solution to your problems, which lies in getting rid of those bogus beliefs.

2. *Isn't Three Minute Therapy just common sense?*

When people refer to "common sense," they are usually thinking of truths which everyone accepts without argument. "Common sense" is what everyone "knows" already. But some beliefs considered to be "common sense" are wrong; at one time it was considered common sense that the earth was flat and that iron ships would not float.

Some things in Three Minute Therapy are contrary to present-day "common sense." To judge by TV shows and movies, a great many people "know" that a stressful childhood experience can be forgotten yet can still influence your behavior in ways that you don't understand; these people also "know" that by remembering and reliving that forgotten childhood trauma, you can become better able to cope with difficulties. But this commonsense "knowledge" is mistaken. No forgotten event in your past can possibly upset you. You may, however, upset yourself by trying to remember some supposedly forgotten event and then dwelling morbidly on it.

There are many other bits of "common sense" or "folk wisdom" which are just plain false. To mention only a few of the popular fallacies we have already mentioned, it's widely believed that a certain amount of anxiety or "stage fright" is helpful to a public speaker, that students will learn more if they feel better about themselves, and that the *only* way to terminate a habit of excessive drinking is by becoming a total abstainer. All these popular beliefs, and many others, are mistaken.

Although some ideas that pass for present-day "common sense" are false, others are true. But this does not mean that the best solution to emotional or behavioral problems is obvious. If you ask a plumber to explain how he tackles a leaky water pipe and why, his explanation will not astound you by its daring leaps of imagination. Every piece of his explanation will sound like common sense, yet knowing which bits of common sense to put together in a particular situation is a skill that requires application and learning. No one would be able, merely by thinking about the truths of common sense, to figure out for themselves all the techniques and practical skills needed to be a plumber. It's the same with Three Minute Therapy.

3. *Three Minute Therapy denies that certain things are awful, terrible, or horrible. But some things really are bad. Dying slowly of AIDS or having your family killed by terrorists really are dreadful prospects to have to face.*

We don't dispute that such things are very bad, nor do we deny that people strongly prefer these things not to happen to them. It is rational to take steps to make such possibilities less likely. But in demanding that they absolutely MUST not happen, you would be asking of the Universe something that it cannot deliver. Sadly, such things do happen to people, and it is both unreasonable and harmful to believe that they MUST not.

4. *People are the way they are. Since I've been this way as long as I can remember, I must be a hopeless case. It must be a deep-seated part of my constitution, so obviously psychotherapy is going to be ineffective.*

People do change in ways that diminish their problems quite dramatically. Drunks and drug addicts do sometimes graduate from heavy to moderate, manageable consumption, or complete abstinence. Long-time procrastinators can change their habits and become far less procrastinating than most. People who suffer crippling anxiety for years do sometimes become quite optimistic and carefree. Victims of phobias lose their fears. Unhappy obese people become happily and permanently slim.

The fact that you have behaved a certain way many times in the past does not prove that you are destined always to behave that way.

5. *Three Minute Therapy says that feelings come from thinking, and undesirable feelings can be eliminated by changing one's thinking. But this can't be true. For example, I feel terribly hurt because Terry, the person I love, has rejected me. I know that there's no reason to think I need Terry's love—I'm fully aware that I don't become a worthless person if Terry rejects me. I have no illusions, yet I still feel awful!*

The thinking that causes your upset may not be obvious to you; it may not be what you think you think. This is not because your thinking is "unconscious" or disguised.

It's simply that part of our thinking is automatic or "knee-jerk."

Imagine yourself sitting next to a swimming pool that has a high diving board. As you watch others dive off the high board, you "know" that it's safe to jump. You decide to give it a try. You climb up the ladder to the high board and cautiously walk to the end. Now you glance down and think how high up you are. You start thinking: "it's so far down. What if I'm hurt? I MUST have a guarantee I won't be."

Your heart starts pounding, your skin starts perspiring profusely. You timidly back off and climb back down the ladder.

What happened here? Safe by the side of the pool, you "know" that you can probably jump from the top board without being hurt, and that it is folly to demand a guarantee certifying that you will survive. But when you're on the high board, looking down at the water far below, then you "know" that without an iron-clad guarantee, the risk of jumping would be "awful."

You evidently have two contradictory beliefs, and the stronger of these two beliefs is responsible for your fear. That's why Three Minute Therapy emphasizes that mere casual assent or lip-service to the "correct" belief is not enough.

> *I'm sorry, I just can't accept that. You're telling me that I can believe two contradictory things at the same time. But surely what the example of the high diving board really shows is that an emotion (fear) can outweigh a belief.*

O.K., let's think about a different example then. Suppose that, after driving a car for years in the U.S., you move to Britain, where they drive on the left. You may "know" that everyone in Britain drives on the left, yet you may still slip into supposing that they drive on the right. Every year several American tourists in London are killed or injured because they forget what they "know" and step off the curb into the path of a car.

Notice that emotion is not an issue here. Your assumption, or habit of thought, or deep-seated belief that everyone drives on the right is not an emotion. You do not feel excited or agitated about which side of the road people drive on in London. In the jargon of psychologists, this is a cognitive rather than an emotive matter. It's a way of thinking that you fall into when you are inattentive—until you have trained yourself to think the other way.

So you may, when you are asked to consider the matter seriously, agree that there is no law of nature requiring that your beloved Terry love you in return. In such lucid moments, you "know" that this is correct. But when you are no longer giving this issue your full attention, you may lapse into supposing that Terry MUST love you, and it's the end of the world if Terry doesn't. You may be constantly telling yourself—whenever you're not critically analyzing the matter, and that's most of the time—that Terry *has* to love you, that it would be terrible, horrible, awful, or dreadful if Terry didn't love you. So some such thought could be the "must" that you use to upset yourself (or it could, of course, be a different "must"—for example: that you MUST get every important thing you would like to get).

In this book we call such a deep-seated assumption as that your chair will support you, that everyone drives on the right, and that Terry MUST love you a "belief." It's convenient in therapy to have a simple term that doesn't change. But if you want to call it something other than "belief"—"assumption," "attitude," "perspective," or "mindset,"—that's fine.

6. *I tried doing a Three Minute Exercise to help me with my depression. But now I seem to be just as depressed as before. What went wrong?*

There are several possibilities, for example:

First, as we have said, it's usually not very effective to just "do it in your head." It's far better to do something active, such as writing the exercise out in full. Maybe you didn't do the exercise actively enough.

Second, you may have been disputing the "wrong" irrational belief. Here's a case where this happened with a client. Francisco wrote the following Three Minute Exercise:

A. (**A**ctivating event): I have now been unemployed for six months.

B. (irrational **B**elief): I SHOULD have a job by now, and since I don't, this proves what a useless bum I am.

C. (emotional **C**onsequences): Depression.

At D, Francisco vigorously disputed the above B, and at E he elaborated several reasons why not having a job did not make him a useless bum. Yet (at F) he continued to feel as melancholy as he had before—his "feeling" did not change.

It subsequently emerged that Francisco's problem was discomfort disturbance ("Must" #3: a demand on the conditions of one's life or on "the Universe"), not ego disturbance ("Must" #1: a demand on oneself). Francisco was not upset, as he had at first thought, because he was putting himself down, but instead because he was railing against his circumstances. The correct "B" for Francisco was: "Life

MUST not be so unfair to me, when everyone else I know has work. I can't stand it!"

As soon as Francisco had worked out and practiced a Three Minute Exercise to combat *this* irrational belief, his depression began to lift.

A third possibility is that you're not making your comments at the E stage convincing enough. The more you write at E, contradicting your "must," the more persuasive you will tend to make E. To safeguard against the possibility of doing too little at E, make it a rule to write at least five statements at E.

Fourth, it is harmful to demand that anything MUST occur the way you want it, and this includes your Three Minute Exercises. It's best not to think "I MUST overcome my problem right now, once and for all. This Three Minute Exercise has GOT TO succeed." If you think like this, you may create a Secondary Disturbance (see chapter 13) which tends to block you from getting at your Primary Disturbance.

*7. Isn't it authentically human to have feelings like anger and depression?*

Sure, and it's authentically human to suffer from toothache or appendicitis. Such feelings as anger and depression are virtually always self-defeating, authentically human or not.

Of course, it's your perfect right to hold on to your anger or depression, for whatever reasons you wish. However, we recommend that you weigh all the advantages and disadvantages before you decide to do so.

If you think it's somehow virtuous to feel wretched, go ahead. But after all, it's also authentically human to strive incessantly to improve your condition.

8. *I have been working conscientiously at my Three Minute Exercises, and I have been facing my feared situations more. But my anxiety has diminished only very slightly. How can that be?*

One likely explanation is that your A's have been increasing as your harmful B's have been diminishing—and precisely *because* your B's have been diminishing. In other words, you may be facing more feared situations, with greater frequency, because your Three Minute Exercises have been working. So, although you are just as anxious, or almost as anxious, you have made progress in changing your behavior.

Matthew feared committing himself in a love relationship. His "must" was: "I MUST not be trapped in a relationship that has gone sour." Because of this, he did almost nothing to meet women or develop relationships. But then in therapy he started to combat this "must," and went through the following progression: he began to meet more women; he started dating; he formed an exclusive relationship; he moved in with his partner; they got married; they bought a house; his wife became pregnant. As his B decreased, his A increased, consequently for several months his C did not diminish much.

Matthew was actually making steady progress, reducing but not eliminating his fear of commitment. As this fear diminished, he allowed himself to increase his actual commitment to his relationship. Matthew continued to work on his unreasonable fear of commitment after his wife had become pregnant. Before the child was born, Matthew did report a dramatic reduction in his anxiety about the relationship.

9. *Three Minute Therapy sounds heartless and calculating. I don't sense any real love and caring.*

Three Minute Therapy *works*. That's the point.

*That last answer proves you're heartless and calculating!*

True compassion and caring calls for an approach that really helps people with their suffering, as Three Minute Therapy does. It can only do harm to encourage people to wallow in their victimhood and self-pity.

10. *Three Minute Therapy sounds as if it might destroy the extremes of emotion—the summits as well as the valleys. But it's better to experience the lows and the highs than to be stable and rational all the time, and miss out on ecstatic peaks.*

*Some* kinds of peaks will indeed cease or diminish. Certain kinds of elation or euphoria are associated with cycles of desperate urgency to satisfy your "musts."

But truly satisfying peaks tend to become "higher" and more frequent if misery is reduced. If your everyday average is an absorbed contentment, your "peaks" will be taller and more commonplace than if your everyday average is gloom and foreboding. For example, if you eliminate fear from love-making, the moments of extreme pleasure will tend to become more frequent and more intense. Or if you eliminate fear from your public speaking, the amount of actual positive joy you get out of making presentations will increase.

However, these satisfying "highs" tend to be the natural outgrowth of an adequate level of contentment and enjoyment. Truly happy individuals are not obsessed all the time with how much joy they can extract from every moment. They are often absorbed in what they are doing, without giving a thought to their moods. Being preoccupied with seeking a "high" is not an effective way to become happy.

11. *I have read that scientists are now showing how moods and emotions are generated by the brain. Doesn't this mean that emotional problems are genetically determined and can only be treated effectively by medication?*

Our brain chemistry, considerably influenced by our genes, does affect our emotional states. But we can learn ways to improve our thinking, feeling, and behaving. This does not contradict the existence of genetic influences.

Consider the ability to play the piano. Millions of people set out to learn the piano. They vary considerably in the level of skill they attain. One important factor in determining who will become a pianist as brilliant as Horowitz is genetic predisposition. Yet almost anyone can learn to play the piano passably well, anyone who can play can improve by more practice, and Horowitz himself could never have become a great pianist, or even a mediocre pianist, if he had never had lessons.

It's the same with other skills, such as skating, tennis, or calculating the odds in a game of poker. There are genetic differences which mean that, with any skill, some people can learn it more easily than other people. But anyone can improve his performance at these activities by practice.

No doubt some individuals have a predisposition to depression, or anxiety, or shyness, or anger, and struggle all their lives against these tendencies, whereas other people are naturally able to avoid these problems comparatively easily.

Research has shown that psychotherapy along the lines of Three Minute Therapy (but not the Freudian-derived style of therapy) does work. For example, some studies indicate that cognitive-behavioral therapy works *better* than antidepressant drugs as a treatment for depression (see the article by Rush, Beck, Kovacs, and Hollan, listed in the bibliography).

By the way, although your brain chemistry may affect your feelings, your thoughts and feelings may also affect your brain chemistry. If you habitually think gloomy thoughts, for instance, you may gradually modify your brain chemistry so that you find it harder to think optimistic thoughts. Your brain is not entirely "hard-wired"; it is partly "programmable" by your chosen "philosophy of life."

12. *One method can't possibly work for everyone. People are so different!*

By a "method" do you mean the *overall approach*, or do you mean the *specific techniques* within that approach? If you mean the overall approach, then Three Minute Therapy can indeed work for anyone capable of reading and understanding this book, just as the theory of ballistics will work for all moving objects—golf balls or space shuttles.

The specific techniques vary according to the individuals' problems. Three Minute Therapy offers not just one technique for all problems, but a range of techniques adapted to individual circumstances.

13. *How can I make myself do the Three Minute Exercises?*

I take it this means you acknowledge that doing the Three Minute Exercises would be valuable for you, would help you to attain your goals, and have a happier life. Yet you are not doing the exercises.

Your problem is probably procrastination. Study chapter 6 in this book. Then, write out a list of the disadvantages of remaining disturbed as a consequence of not doing the Three Minute Exercises, then vividly and thoughtfully read through this list three times a day.

# The Five Unique Advantages of REBT

Albert Ellis, who has been called "the Copernicus of psychotherapy," introduced "Rational Therapy," later to be called Rational Emotive Behavior Therapy (REBT) in 1955, a radical change from all the traditional therapies popular at the time. *Three Minute Therapy* is soundly based on Ellis's REBT.

Many other therapies have been devised since 1955, incorporating some but not all elements of REBT, and all these therapies are now classed as forms of Cognitive-Behavioral Therapy (CBT). All these therapies may do some good, but we believe that the original REBT possesses some unique advantages over other types of CBT.

All types of CBT maintain that human emotions and behavior are predominantly generated by ideas, beliefs, attitudes, and thinking, not by events themselves. Consequently changing your thinking can lead to emotional and behavioral change.

There are major differences between REBT and other types of CBT. Here are the five most important ones:

## 1. PHILOSOPHY

REBT addresses the philosophical basis of emotional disturbance as well as the distorted cognitions (the sole focus of some kinds of CBT), which makes it more powerful. As you uproot your absolutistic demands, your cognitive distortions get corrected.

For example, suppose you plan to ask someone for a second date and you're feeling anxious. You tell yourself, "She didn't talk or smile much on our first date. I know she's not interested." Since there are multiple other explanations for her reserved behavior, which you don't know by her actions, much CBT calls this conclusion "mind-reading" and dismisses it as a "cognitive distortion."

Instead, REBT looks at the underlying reason you jump to this conclusion, for example telling yourself, "I *absolutely need* her acceptance and if she rejects me this would be *awful*, I *could not stand it* and it proves I'm a *loser* who'll never succeed with any woman." Giving up your dire need for acceptance would not only ameliorate your fears of rejection in future dating situations but in virtually all interpersonal interactions. Just avoiding mind-reading proves to be a lot more limited.

REBT identifies three core demands fueling cognitive distortions and underlying emotional disturbance: 1. "Because I strongly *prefer* to, I *absolutely must* do well in life and get the approval of significant others or else I'm *no good*," 2. "Because I keenly *desire* it, others *absolutely must* treat me well or else they're *no good*," and 3. "Because I passionately *wish* it, life *absolutely must* go well and or else it's *no good*." These demands create anxiety, depression, guilt, anger, resentment, procrastination, and addictions.

The simple yet profound philosophical solution involves Unconditional Acceptance (UA): unconditionally accepting yourself with your flaws, unconditionally accepting others with their imperfections, and accepting life unconditionally with its discomfort, hassles, and unfairness.

## 2. SECONDARY DISTURBANCE

REBT highlights the significance of Secondary Disturbance. Disturbing yourself about your disturbance is often the major factor in life-long (endogenous) depression, severe anxiety, and panic attacks. Most CBT ignores Secondary Disturbance. For example, you feel anxious about appearing anxious when requesting the date. You are worrying about worrying.

### 3. UNCONDITIONAL SELF-ACCEPTANCE (USA)

REBT presents an elegant solution to the self-esteem problem. It teaches unconditional self-acceptance (USA) rather than any type of self-rating.

Most CBT therapists focus on boosting their clients' self-esteem by reinforcing some of their positive qualities. This strategy has many pitfalls including returning to low self-esteem when you do poorly, making invidious comparisons to others, avoiding risk-taking, smug-complacency, and preoccupation with proving, rather than enjoying, yourself.

Adopting USA and avoiding the self-rating trap escapes the many problems caused by self-rating. USA is the philosophy of unconditionally accepting yourself as the imperfect human you are, whether you do well or poorly, or whether others love or hate you. If you get fired, for example, it may be okay to rate your job performance as poor, but it's best not to overgeneralize to conclude that you're a poor or worthless person. If you avoid that trap, you're then able to evaluate your deficient (and positive) behaviors, to focus on how to improve in the future.

### 4. HELPFUL NEGATIVE EMOTIONS

REBT is unique among CBT therapies in differentiating between self-destructive, inappropriate negative emotions and helpful, appropriate negative emotions. Not all negative emotions are harmful. Anxiety, depression, and anger are examples of harmful negative emotions; intense sadness, deep sorrow, great concern, and regret are instances of harmless and sometimes even helpful negative emotions.

For example, if you feel anxious about arriving five minutes late for an appointment, this is an inappropriate negative emotion because, in part, it comes from rigid, absolutistic thinking characterized by demands (*musts, shoulds, have tos*: "I *absolutely must* never be late for an appointment"). Alternatively, if you feel intensely sad, you cry, grieve, and mourn the loss of a loved one, these are appropriate negative emotions. They come from passionate desires and preferences such as, "I strongly *wish* my lover had not died, how very, very sad and most "unfortunate."

## 5. ALL ANGER IS UNHELPFUL

Most types of CBT view some anger as healthy and appropriate. Counter to this, REBT maintains that all anger has a commanding and condemning, dictatorial, philosophical core. This can be expressed as "others *absolutely must* treat me well or else they're *no good* and deserve to roast in hell." This philosophy is unhelpful, feels bad, and can sometimes be quite destructive. Even in mild forms, this perspective is inappropriate.

REBT teaches individuals effective assertiveness, problem-solving, and other appropriate alternatives to anger. Although other kinds of CBT usually also teach assertiveness, this in itself fails to uproot the philosophical root of anger.

Because of these five distinctive features, missing from most kinds of CBT, REBT therapy tends to be quicker and briefer than the other forms of CBT.

# Bibliotherapy: Other Helpful Reading

The following bibliography includes all the books and articles we have mentioned in this book, plus a few others we recommend.

Baumeister, Roy F., Joseph M. Boden, and Laura Smart. "Relation of Threatened Egotism to Violence and Aggression: The Dark Side of High Self-Esteem." *Psychological Review,* Vol. 103, No. 1 (February, 1996), pp. 5–33.

Bufe, Charles. *Alcoholics Anonymous: Cult or Cure?* San Francisco: See Sharp Press, 1991.

Claxton, Guy. *The Heart of Buddhism.* San Francisco: Aquarian Press, 1992.

Edelstein, Michael R. "The ABC's of Rational-Emotive Therapy: Pitfalls of Going from D to E." *Rational Living*, 11: 1 (1976), pp. 12–13.

Edelstein, Michael R., and Tommy Bateman, "The REBT Advocates." http://threeminutetherapy.com/podcasts/ (videos)

————. "Educational Audiotape Approaches to Short-term Weight Loss." See *Dissertation Abstracts International,* 41:8 (1981), pp. 3158–59.

Ellis, Albert. *Anger: How to Live With It and Without It.* Secaucus, NJ: Citadel Press, 1977.

————. *Better, Deeper, and More Enduring Brief Therapy: The Rational Emotive Behavior Therapy Approach.* New York: Brunner/Mazel, 1995.

————. *How to Live with a Neurotic.* Rev. edn. North Hollywood: Wilshire, 1975.

————. *How to Master Your Fear of Flying.* New York: Institute for Rational-Emotive Therapy, 1972.

Ellis, Albert, Michael Abrams, and Lidia Dengelegi, *The Art and Science of Rational Eating.* New York: Barricade Books, 1992.

Ellis, Albert, and Robert A. Harper, *A Guide to Successful Marriage.* North Hollywood: Wilshire, 1961.

————. *A New Guide to Rational Living.* North Hollywood: Wilshire, 1975.

Ellis, Albert, and Pat Hunter. *Why Am I Always Broke?* New York: Carol, 1991.

Ellis, Albert, and William J. Knaus. *Overcoming Procrastination.* New York: Signet, 1977.

Ellis, Albert, and Art Lange. *How to Keep People from Pushing Your Buttons.* New York: Carol, 1994.

Ellis, Albert, and Emmett Velten. *When AA Doesn't Work for You: Rational Steps for Quitting Alcohol.* New York: Barricade Books, 1992.

Epictetus. *The Handbook of Epictetus.* Indianapolis: Hackett, 1983.

# Bibliotheraphy: Other Helpful Reading

Eysenck, Michael W. *Happiness: Facts and Myths.* Hove, U.K.: Erlbaum, 1990.

Fox, Vince. *Addiction, Change, and Choice: The New View of Alcoholism.* Tucson: See Sharp Press, 1994.

Frankl, Viktor E. *Man's Search for Meaning.* New York: Washington Square Press, 1966.

Krauthammer, Charles. "Education: Doing Bad and Feeling Good." *Time,* 5th February, 1990.

Peele, Stanton, and Archie Brodsky, with M. Arnold. *The Truth about Addiction and Recovery: The Life-Process Program for Outgrowing Destructive Habits.* New York: Simon and Schuster, 1991.

Rahula, Walpola. *What the Buddha Taught.* Rev. edn. New York: Grove Weidenfeld, 1974.

Rush, A.J., A. Beck, M. Kovacs, and S. Hollan. "Comparative Efficacy of Cognitive Therapy and Pharmacotherapy in the Treatment of Depressed Outpatients." *Cognitive Therapy and Research,* Vol. 1, No. 1 (March, 1977), pp. 17–38.

Steele, David Ramsay. "Partial Recall." *Liberty,* March 1994.

Szasz, Thomas. *The Untamed Tongue: A Dissenting Dictionary.* Chicago: Open Court, 1990.

Trimpey, Jack. *Rational Recovery: The New Cure for Substance Addiction.* New York: Simon and Schuster, 1996.

# Index

demands, irrational.
*See* musts
depression, 7, 35–37, 44–
45, 62–63, 85–89, 109–
124, 172, 216, 222, 224–
225, 234, 241–242, 245–
246  and daily mood rat-
ings 117; and relation-
ships 115–116; and self-
downing 85–86; and self-
rating 39–41, 44–46; gen-
erated by beliefs 7, 35, 44,
59, 62–63; genetic predisposition 245; not deter-
mined by the objective
situation alone 3–4, 30–
32, 119–120
diets, 125
difficult people, 75
disadvantages, method of
enumerating, 23, 52, 63,
73–75, 127–130, 170,
176, 212, 242
discomfort disturbance,
219, 232, 241. *See al-
so* anxiety, discomfort
Disputing musts (gen-
eral), 9–13, 28, 35,
49–51, 74–75, 226
Disputing musts (spe-
cific cases), 11, 20,
35, 44–45, 52, 62, 73,
81–82, 87, 92, 97,

122, 139–140, 150–
152, 157–158, 163,
167, 183, 188, 199,
210, 220. *See* Three
Minute Exercises
(specific cases)
divorce, 57, 65, 67, 72, 80,
94
Dole, Bob, 204
drinking. *See* compulsive
(or excessive) drinking
drugs, 88–89, 126, 179–
193, 237

eating disorders. *See* overeating
Effective new thinking
(general), 11, 112, 183
Effective new thinking
(specific cases), 20, 35,
45, 52, 62, 73, 82, 88,
92, 97, 122, 152, 158,
163, 167, 188, 199, 210,
220
ego disturbance, 219, 229,
232, 241
elation, 38, 244
Ellis, Albert, ix–x, xi, 3, 6,
61
embarrassment, 72, 81, 196
emotional consequences.
*See* Consequences, emo-
tional

emotional problem (distinct from practical problem), 30–31, 56–58, 70, 72, 86, 121, 230

Emotional problems, 7–10, 48, 88; causation of, 28, 31, 49, 119–120, 148, 236. *See also* anxiety; anger; depression; guilt; self-pity; shame; Three Minute Exercises

Epictetus, 1, 48

etiquette, 195, 202

excuses, 107, 189, 190, 222

fallible human beings 46, 62, 153, 156, 158

fear, 4, 15–19, 23, 26–28, 91, 136, 144, 152–154, 157, 159, 161, 168, 175, 177, 186, 196, 200, 200–205, 209, 215–221, 223–224, 227–228, 238–239, 243–244

meter 215; of being afraid 215–218, 224–225; of being inadvertently impregnated 15; of being sued 16; of catching AIDS from food 19–21; of committing a violent crime 16–17; of crossing bridges 228–229; of

crowds 223; of doing something outrageous in public 17; of dying while asleep 17; of earthquakes 18; of elevators 154–159, 216, 227; of examinations 3; of financial loss 30; of flying 18–19, 175; of ghosts 215–216; of having a sex-change operation 15; of heights 216, 228; of losing one's mind 9, 145, 153; of momentary anxiety 221; of hugging impropriety 195–213; of objects falling out of airplanes 15; of sharks in the swimming pool 15–28; of social situations 195–200, 204–206; of swallowing loudly 200–201; of talking to a bank teller 204; of waiting in line 143, 145, 223;

*See also* anxiety; panic attacks; public speaking anxiety; shyness; worry

Feeling, new (general), 12

Feeling, new (specific cases), 21, 36, 45, 52, 63, 74, 82, 88, 93, 97, 123, 140, 152, 159, 164, 167, 183, 188, 200, 221, 226

feelings: come from thinking, 1–3, 28, 31, 48–49,
56, 119–120, 148 174; of
being overwhelmed 86,
166, 225; of worthless-
ness 24, 32, 36, 43, 45,
50, 86, 110, 118–119,
133, 167, 173, 175, 177,
198, 210, 216, 219, 238;
*See* self-downing. *See also* Fielding, Henry, 161
financial problems.
 *See* money problems
flashcards, 197
Frankl, Viktor E., 120, 200–
21
free will, 52, 73, 82
Freud, Sigmund, 3–4, 91,
116, 147, 203, 218, 245.
*See also* psychoanalytic
(Freudian) method of
therapy
 Freudian psychotherapy.
*See* psychoanalytic
(Freudian) method of
therapy
frustration tolerance, vii, 33,
87, 127, 135, 137, 139,
173, 177

Gamblers Anonymous, 179
 genetic influences, 186,
206, 245

goals, personal, 8–9, 22, 92,
139, 174, 234, 246; unre-
alistic 8–9, 11, 58
"got tos". *See* musts
guarantee. *See* certain-
ty, demand for
guilt, 7, 86, 91, 129, 137,
165, 172, 175, 223–224.
*See also* shame

happiness, 233
 hassles, life consists of, 24,
25, 62, 122–124, 137,
167, 172–173
high frustration tolerance.
*See* frustration tolerance
Hitler, Adolf, 179
Hollan, S., 246
Holmes, Oliver Wendell,
Sr., 29
 homework assign-
ment (therapy), 61,
212
Horowitz, Vladimir, 245
 household chores, 59, 95–
97
*How to Live with a Neurotic*
(Ellis), 61
Hume, David, 120
humor, 78, 120, 200–201,
218

imagery, 107–108, 140–141, 211–213

imperfect human beings. *See* fallible human beings

impotence, 235

indecisiveness, 163–164

individuals' different responses to similar circumstances, 3, 47–48, 105–106

individuals' power to control their lives, 4, 192, 237–240. *See also* free will

inertia, tendency to, 97–99

insomnia, 90, 112, 137; oversleeping, 112

intimidation, 42

job-related problems, 21–25, 31, 42, 79, 85–86, 99–101, 120–121, 141, 169–170, 175–176, 190, 209, 216, 220, 241

jogging, 37–39

keeping up with the Joneses, 173–175

Keillor, Garrison, 204

Kovacs, M., 246

lateness, persistent, 71–73, 78–79, 121

Limbaugh, Rush, 204

list of reasons why "must" is false, 23, 132, 149

loneliness, 177

love, 6, 55–57, 67, 69, 78, 111, 172, 203, 204, 213, 217, 234, 238, 240, 243–244

low frustration tolerance. *See* frustration tolerance

*Man's Search for Meaning* (Frankl), 120

Mantle, Mickey, 182

marital problems, 37, 51, 53, 56

marriage. *See* marital problems

Mathis, Johnny, 204

medication (for emotional problems), 245

memories, unconscious. *See* unconscious mind

Milton, John, 109

mind-reading, 250

moderate drinking, 180, 182–183, 238

money management, 168

money problems, 31, 35–36, 161–177

Montaigne, Michel Eyquem de, 15

Monty Python, 233

Moral Rearmament, 179

Mozart, Wolfgang, 37, 151

Must #1 (demands on oneself) 8, 49–50, 219, 241

Must #2 (demands on other people) 8, 49–50

Must #3 (demands on the universe) 8, 50–51, 219, 241

musts (demands), 5–10, 12–13, 22, 28, 31, 43–44, 49–51, 56, 67, 73, 80–81, 97, 112, 124, 130, 134–135, 147–151, 153, 157, 162, 166, 172–173, 197, 206, 225–226, 230, 244; cause behavioral problems, 94–96, 236; cause emotional problems, 28, 79–80, 229, 236; convincing oneself of falseness of 150; identification of 5–6, 9–10, 49–51, 60, 224–225, 240–242; replacing with preferences, 12, 42–44, 65–67, 148–149, 157; three kinds of 49–50; *See also* Disputing musts; Must #1; Must #2; Must #3

musty thinking, 9, 13, 22, 86, 101, 110, 112–118, 123, 127, 147, 166, 182, 193, 207, 218, 226

myths, 115

nagging, 65

negative emotions, not always unhelpful, 261–62

negative thinking, 127

New behavior (specific cases), 88, 93, 97, 140, 164, 167,

New feeling (general), 12, 183

New feeling (specific cases), 21, 36, 45, 52, 63, 74, 82, 88, 93, 97, 123, 140, 152, 159, 164, 167, 188, 200, 211, 221

No Future Regrets method, 89, 102

No pain, no gain, 91–93, 136

O'Brien, Conan, 204

obsessing and preoccupation, 39, 68, 119, 206

organizational skills, 100–101, 103

orgasmic dysfunction, 235

Overeaters Anonymous, 179

overeating, 7, 88–89, 125–141

Oxford Group Movement, 179, 192

panic attacks, 143–159
paradoxical intention, 200–201
Peele, Stanton, 182
penalties. *See* rewards and penalties as a way of changing behavior
perfectionism, 35, 43, 65, 73, 111
personality questionnaire, 126
phobias. *See* fear
physical symptoms, 144, 146, 153
pondering, without anxiety, 26–27
"positive" attitude, 33
practical problem (as distinct from emotional problem), 30–31, 39, 56, 58, 70, 72, 86, 103, 121, 201, 205, 207, 213, 225, 230, 235
practice (acquiring a skill), viii, 12–14, 24, 26, 35, 41, 45, 79, 90–91, 93, 96, 99, 100, 108, 115, 117, 124, 128–129, 136, 139, 141, 151–153, 157–159, 163, 189, 198, 201, 207, 212–213, 220, 227, 234, 242, 245

preferences (contrasted with demands), viii, 7–9, 13, 31, 66–67, 147–149, 157, 234
Premack, David, 106
Premack's Principle, 106–107
primary disturbance (primary problem), 216, 218, 223–225, 230–232, 242
prioritizing, 102
Problem Separation Technique, 30, 230, 235
procrastination, 7, 85–108, 234–235, 246; reasonable 89
progressive relaxation. *See* Three Minute Relaxation
Proust, Marcel, 27
psychoanalytic (Freudian) method of therapy, 91, 116, 203, 218, 245. *See also* unconscious mind
public speaking anxiety, 6, 209–213, 244

Rational Emotive Behavior Therapy (Rational Emotive Therapy), vii, ix, 6, 192; *See also* Ellis, Albert; Three Minute Therapy

Three Minute Judo, 97–98
Three Minute Penalties, 104
Three Minute Procrastination Buster, 98, 104
Three Minute Refutations, 189–191
Three Minute Relaxation, 206–207
Three Minute Therapy, 5, 7, 9, 13–14, 63, 156, 191–193, 201, 234–239, 243–246. *See also* Ellis, Albert; Rational Emotive Behavior Therapy; Three Minute Exercises
Three Minute Wake-Up Imagery, 107–108
Three Second Knockouts, 123–124
Tolstoy, Leo, 215
12 Steps, 180, 184

uncertainty. *See* certainty, demand for
unconditional acceptance, 45, 188

unconditional self-acceptance, 45
unconscious mind, 3–5, 91, 116, 136, 146. *See also* psychoanalytic (Freudian) method of therapy

vicious circles in relationships, 53–63, 78
victimhood. *See* self-pity
violence, 7, 68

Walters, Barbara, 204
War on Drugs, 185
weight loss. *See* overeating
Weight Watchers, 88
Wilde, Oscar, 85
worry, 5, 15–28, 42, 145, 155, 195, 199, 201, 215–217, 234. *See also* anxiety; fears
worst-case scenario, 24, 150, 161–162, 173, 197

# *About the Authors*

DR. MICHAEL R. EDELSTEIN has a telephone, Skype, and in-person therapy practice in San Francisco and Tiburon, California. With co-author David Ramsay Steele he wrote *Therapy Breakthrough,* a history and critique of the psychotherapy movement from Sigmund Freud to Albert Ellis. *Stage Fright,* co-authored with Mick Berry, includes interviews with Robin Williams, Jason Alexander, Melissa Etheridge, Maya Angelou, and others, relating their personal experiences and wisdom in coping with performance anxiety. His book *Rational Drinking: How to Live Happily With or Without Alcohol* presents concepts, tools, and strategies for overcoming compulsive drinking. He has a YouTube channel, "The REBT Advocates," with Tommy Bateman.

In his practice, Dr. Edelstein specializes in the treatment of anxiety, depression, relationship problems, and addictions, and is one of the few practitioners of REBT in the San Francisco Bay Area. He was also the San Francisco SMART Recovery Professional Advisor and occasionally leads meetings in San Francisco.

Dr. Edelstein lectures nationally and internationally, appears on radio and television, and is published in psychological journals. He wrote the advice column, "Ask Dr. Mike," which appeared in the Mensa San Francisco "Intelligencer" and "In the Know."

Dr. Edelstein was a Training Supervisor and Fellow of the Albert Ellis Institute. He is a diplomate in Cognitive-Behavioral Therapy from the National Association of Cognitive-Behavioral Therapists, and is on its Board of Advisors. He is Past President of the Association for Behavioral and Cognitive Therapy. He is a Certified Sex Therapist and has served as a Consulting Psychologist for the National Save-A-Life League, Inc., the oldest suicide prevention center in the United States.

DAVID RAMSAY STEELE wrote the iconoclastic and controversial book about George Orwell, *Orwell Your Orwell: A Worldview on the Slab* (2017). His other books include *Atheism Explained* (2008) and *From Marx to Mises* (1992). He was the 2017 recipient of the Thomas S. Szasz Award for Outstanding Contributions to the Cause of Civil Liberties. He frequently lectures at the College of Complexes, Chicago's free speech forum, and many of his talks can be found on YouTube.

Also by the authors of Three Minute Therapy:

# Therapy Breakthrough

*Why Some Psychotherapies Work Better than Others*

MICHAEL R, EDELSTEIN, PH.D., RICHARD K. KUJOTH, ED.D., DAVID RAMSAY STEELE, PH.D.

Like no other book you have ever read, *Therapy Breakthrough* explains clearly and vividly just what goes on in psychotherapy, why there are so many different systems of psychotherapy which disagree with one another, where these different schools of therapy came from, why psychotherapy is continually misrepresented in popular culture, and why, despite all this, psychotherapy gets good results, is improving all the time, and is superior to drugs in helping you solve your problems.

*"If you have a rational mind—or would like to have one—*Therapy Breakthrough *will be indispensable in helping you see how Cognitive Behavioral therapy can be used to make your life happier and healthier."*

—WARREN FARRELL, PH.D., bestselling author of *Women Can't Hear What Men Don't Say* (1999)

*"Prepare to embark on a rollicking yet highly informative journey through the intense world of psychotherapy! In engaging style the authors, who respectfully dedicate their book to the memory of my beloved husband, present much substantial information, as well as making some assertions which may spark healthy controversy."*

—DEBBIE JOFFE ELLIS, PH.D., co-author (with Albert Ellis) of *All Out!* (2010) and co-author (with Albert Ellis) of *Rational Emotive Behavior Therapy* (2011)

"Therapy Breakthrough *is a bold and instantly readable primer on the seismic shift in psychotherapy as seen from within the profession—and a helpful reminder of what is at the core of modern therapeutic techniques. It's also a fun read!"*

—NANDO PELUSI, PH.D., contributing editor for *Psychology Today*

Made in the
USA
Middletown, DE